BRAVE HEADS

BRAVE HEADS

HOW TO LEAD A SCHOOL WITHOUT SELLING YOUR SOUL

DAVE HARRIS
EDITED BY IAN GILBERT

Independent Thinking Press

First published by
Independent Thinking Press
Crown Buildings, Bancyfelin, Carmarthen, Wales, SA33 5ND, UK
www.independentthinkingpress.com

Independent Thinking Press is an imprint of Crown House Publishing Ltd.

First published 2012.

Page 124: Extract from *Supporting the Emotional Work of School Leaders* © Belinda Harris has been reproduced with the kind permission of Sage Publications Ltd.
Page 125: Extract from *Leadership Capacity for Lasting School Improvement* © Linda Lambert has been reproduced with the kind permission of ASCD.
Page 127: Extract from *Successful Principal Leadership in Times of Change: An International Perspective* © Christopher Day and Kenneth Leithwood has been reproduced with the kind permission of Springer.
Page 130: Extract is reprinted by permission *from Leading the Learning Organization: Communication and Competencies for Managing Change* by Alan T. Belasen, The State of New York Press, © 2000, State University of New York. All rights reserved.
Page 132: Extract from *Educational Leadership: Culture and Diversity* © Clive Dimmock and Allan Walker has been reproduced with the kind permission of Sage Publications Ltd.
Page 133: Extract from *The Six Secrets of Change* © Michael Fullan has been reproduced with kind permission of John Wiley & Sons Ltd.
Page 134: Hargreaves and Fink extract from *Developing Sustainable Leadership* © Brent Davies has been reproduced with the kind permission of Sage Publications Ltd - Hargreaves & Fink.
Page 136: Extract from *Schooling the Rustbelt Kids: Making the Difference in Changing* Times © Pat Thomson has been reproduced with the kind permission of Trentham Books.
Pages 138, 148 and 152: Extracts from *Schools of Hope: A New Agenda for School Improvement* © Terry Wrigley have been reproduced with the kind permission of Trentham Books.
Page 140: Extract from *System Re-design – 1. The Road to Transformation* © David Hargreaves has been reproduced with the kind permission of SSAT (The Schools Network) Ltd.
Pages 142, 144: Extracts from *Improving Schools from Within: Teachers, Parents and Principals Can Make a Difference* © Roland Barth have been reproduced with the kind permission of John Wiley & Sons Ltd.
Page 145-6: Extract from 'Relations Between Teachers' Approaches to Teaching and Students' Approaches to Learning' © Keith Trigwell, published in *Higher Education* has been reproduced with the kind permission of Springer.
Page 153-4: Extract from *Moral Leadership: Getting to the Heart of School Improvement* © Thomas Sergiovanni has been reproduced with the kind permission of John Wiley & Sons Ltd.
Page 155-6: Extract from *Understanding School Leadership* © Peter Earley and Dick Weindling has been reproduced with the kind permission of Sage Publications Ltd.
Page 156-7: Extract from Summary statement: The Emergent, Cyclical, Double-Helix Model of the Adult Human Biopsychosocial Systems. Handout for a presentation to the Future Society, Boston, MA, 20 May 1981. Copyright NVC Consulting, has been reproduced with kind permission.
Page 158: Reprinted with permission of the publisher. *From Leadership and the New Science* © 2006 Margaret Wheatley, Berrett-Koehler Publishers, Inc. San Francisco, CA. All rights reserved. www.bkconnection.com
Page 160: Extract from *School Improvement for Real* © David Hopkins has been reproduced with the kind permission of Taylor and Francis Books.
Page 161: Extract from *What Great Principals Do Differently: Fifteen Things That Matter Most* © Todd Whittaker has been reproduced with the kind permission of Eye on Education (www.eyeoneducation.com)
Pages 162 and 164: Diagram and extract reproduced with the kind permission of John West-Burnham.
Page 165: Extract from *Visible Learning: A Synthesis of Over 800 Meta-Analyses Relating to Achievement* © John Hattie has been reproduced with the kind permission of Taylor and Francis Books.
Page 168: Extract from *How to Change 5000 Schools: A Practical and Positive Approach for Leading Change at Every Level* © Ben Levin has been reproduced with the kind permission of the Harvard Education Publishing Group.
Page 176: *A Bravery Pledge* © Lynn C. Johnson has been reproduced with the kind permission of the author. www.whisperingangelbooks.com

British Library Cataloguing-in-Publication Data
A catalogue entry for this book is available
from the British Library.

Print ISBN 978-1-78135-048-5
Mobi ISBN 978-1-78135-057-7
ePub ISBN 978-1-78135-058-4

Printed and bound in the UK by
TJ International, Padstow, Cornwall

FOREWORD

I have a friend who is a head teacher at a prestigious school on the coast in Chile. It is his third headship and he has been there nearly two years now. In his office is a daunting gallery of oil paintings of 150 years' worth of headmasters (they are all men) looking down on him each day as he sits at his desk. The combined pressure of all that tradition, expertise and accomplishment frighten the life out of him most days.

Another experienced head teacher I know at a school in England was telling me about the sudden feelings of panic he experiences from time to time. 'I would understand it,' he explained to me, 'if it was on a Sunday evening but this is in the middle of the summer holidays while I'm sitting in my garden!' His anxiety disorder aside, it is the comment about Sunday evenings that is most telling.

Another head teacher I knew (I still know her. It's just that she is no longer a head teacher. It was just a phase she was going through) used to walk around her school pretending she knew what she was doing. 'How would I be acting if I really knew what to do?' is how she used to explain this to herself. She was especially reliant on the 'fake it till you make it' approach when it came to dealing with the school budget and the massive deficit she had inherited. 'What would I do if I knew what I was doing?' It was a strategy that helped her get the school back in the black within 18 months.

It's a challenge being a head teacher. A big one. And unless you're one of those arrogant types who refuses to believe that anything you do could ever go wrong and if it does it's someone else's fault anyway, it's a really scary challenge.

I remember my very first day as an NQT. I bumped into the silver-haired avuncular deputy in the gents. 'Nervous?' he asked. 'Yup,' I said, thinking about all the dreams I had had in the weeks leading up to that day, those sweat-inducing dreams of being in a classroom and not having a clue what was going on as chaos raged around me. 'Yup,' he continued, 'me too. It never leaves you …'

Fear, then, seems to be a staple of life in a school, unlike many other common jobs (but akin to being a burglar according to the controversial Judge Bowers in Teeside recently who seemed impressed with the guts of the serial-burglaring drug addict up before him). Fear. Or F.E.A.R. – F*ck Everything And Run! – as it was once described to me. It takes bravery to overcome fear. If you never experience fear then how can you be brave? When you are a teacher, you have to face your fears and get yourself through every day. When you're a head, you have to get yourself through every day and everyone else as well.

There is a great deal of talk these days about 'super-heads' and the need to succeed at all costs, success often measured solely in exam results and Ofsted headlines. It is a success that can come despite, not as a result of, the staff it would appear, based on what Ofsted chief Sir Michael Wilshaw seems to say, a man who seems to like the 'carrot and stick' approach to motivation using both objects with which to beat teachers. What would the epitome of courage in leadership Sir Ernest Shackleton say about that? At one point during his ill-fated expedition to the South Pole, he confided to the captain of the *Endurance*, Frank Arthur Worsley, 'Thank God I haven't killed one of my men!' to which the loyal captain replied, 'We all know you have worked superhumanly to look after us.' Shackleton's gruff response is revealing when considering what real leadership is about: 'Superhuman effort … isn't worth a damn unless it achieves results.'

I asked a friend of mine, David Hanson who heads up the Independent Association of Prep Schools and a man who has had more than his fair share of educational leadership experience, what his approach was when it came to taking all staff with you as a school leader. Surely you just get rid of the dead weight holding a school back? Isn't that the brave thing for a head to do?

'Relentless support', was his response, a phrase with a professionally pleasing oxymoronic irony to it. You just keep on supporting them until something happens.

Dave Harris displays a similar approach when it comes to bringing the best out of his staff. All his staff. The expectation was that he would come with a scythe and cut down all that was holding back the school from which Nottingham University Samworth Academy or NUSA grew out of. Many saw it as a failing school. Failing the students. Failing the community. Failing itself. Why would you hang on to what and who had been part of that failure?

Not sacking large numbers of people was Dave's second brave act at NUSA. Taking the job was the first. Right from day one, Dave wanted to do it in a way that he felt was the right way, the only way. The pressure on him was purely about results but the job before him, Dave knew, was bigger than that. Focusing on the important things – 'the marathon' activities as he calls it – as well as chasing external goals such as ever-moving floor targets – 'the sprint' activities – took courage. Doing what you feel, deep down, is the right thing to do day after day as the powers that be circle round you like vultures surrounding a peaky-looking zebra takes every ounce of bravery you have and, in this book, Dave is honest about the toll that takes and the roller-coaster ride this approach to leadership really is.

Not that you would know if you ever met him. As Shackleton said, as a leader you keep your fears to yourself: 'You often have to hide from them not only the truth, but your feelings about the truth. You may know that the facts are dead against you, but you mustn't say so.'

This book then is Dave Harris' opportunity to be honest. To share with the reader the stresses and strains of leading a school when you are brave enough to do it the only way you feel is the right way, despite what 'they' say and the pressure to do it 'their' way. In it, he is not telling you what to do as a school leader yourself. Not only is every school different, but every year in every school is different (or at least it should be, if you're being brave about it). Rather he shares his own experiences and the thinking behind them – backed up by some pretty impressive academic research as you might expect from an academy that was the first to have a university as its co-sponsor – to inspire you not only to find your own brave path but to also to have fun doing it.

As Worsley said of Shackleton: 'One would think he had never a care on his mind and he is the life and soul of half the skylarking and fooling in the ship.' After all, as every brave head knows, education is far too important to be taken seriously.

Ian Gilbert
Market Harborough
October 2012

ACKNOWLEDGEMENTS

Brave Leadership can be lonely, but it doesn't have to be. My life is rich; I am surrounded by a wonderful family, great friends and amazing colleagues.

To my wife Esther, and my daughters Bethan and Megan go my deepest thanks; thanks for keeping me grounded, for helping me remember why I do all this and for always believing in me. I love you.

To Mum and Dad, for the richness of support and love you have always given me.

To Ian Gilbert and the ITLers for being there whether we were winning or losing and for always believing we would win in the end!

To Professor Di Birch and Alan Dewar for your generosity of spirit, intellect of mind and unstinting friendship.

To Angela Garry, you are an amazing PA, completely mad of course, but always there to support the journey; even when your own health has been in question NUSA always comes first!

Arjen, you have forever changed the way school meals are thought of – you don't realise how amazing you are.

To Magic Mathew McFall, you have lifted me when I am down more times than you know. How one man can be the centre of so much wonder and positivity is a mystery to me.

To the staff, pupils and governors of NUSA who joined the journey with energy and enthusiasm.

To Willoughby on the Wolds Bowls Club who help me remember that bravery is sometimes switching the phone off!

Finally to the countless head teachers current and past without whose bravery the world would be a poorer place.

CONTENTS

CONTENTS

CONTENTS

INTRODUCTION

1 BRAVERY IS LOOKING THE INSPECTORS IN THE EYE

'Well?' said Laura, my Head of English.

'I'm not allowed to tell you yet,' I croaked, trying to hold back the emotion. 'Not yet but …' My voice trailed away. It was too much to bear. I leant against the doorframe to stop myself from falling, desperately, unsuccessfully, trying to hold back my tears.

Hardly the behaviour of a brave head.

Imagine what would have happened if the inspectors hadn't just given us 'Good' on all four counts! Good for behaviour. Good for teaching. Good for achievement. Good for leadership. Good for overall effectiveness. For such a small word, 'good' can have a very sizeable effect, especially when it was the word that you know you deserved but you feared you would never see.

All the headlines about the new Ofsted inspection regime seemed to suggest that the odds were stacked against them appreciating all that we had achieved. Despite how far we had come in such a short time, despite surpassing our 'floor targets' to make us one of the most improved schools in England, despite so many other successes great and small that were happening each and every day of our journey through the hard work of all our staff, children and the community at large. Despite all of that, I felt the inspectors would come in with their reports already at least partly written, that all our effort would come to nothing and I would be reduced to scanning the *Times Educational Supplement* job pages. The night before the inspectors arrived I emailed a respected friend and described my emotions to him: 'I feel as if I'm going into a football match where the best I can achieve is a draw,' I complained in my pre-inspection blues.

But I was wrong. Delightedly so. They did see what we were achieving and, even more importantly, they saw how we were going about achieving it:

> Senior Leaders have been highly effective in driving up standards, and as a result the quality of teaching has improved and students now make good progress. Since the opening of the academy leaders have been determined to be reflective and researched-based, appreciating the need to make rapid improvement whilst not losing sight of building for long-term success.

My belief in what I felt was the right way forward for this school, and my professional obstinacy in sticking to that path, despite the seemingly endless pressure to do things 'their way', was paying off. Again. Emotions such as elation, depression, hope, despair, the feeling as if you are trying to move a mountain using a toothpick – that is what being a head is all about. Facing those emotions with a sense of self-belief drawn from experience, observation and research, backed up by a gut instinct and applied carefully, methodically and wholeheartedly despite everything that is said and done by those who see things differently – that is what being a brave head is all about. This book is my way of helping you to see that, with bravery, you can achieve practically anything. It is the book I wish I had in my hands in my darkest hours. I hope for you, when you are up against it and especially when you are feeling under pressure to lead a school along a route you know isn't right, that it will act to reassure you and that it will give you the courage to be brave.

> With bravery, you can achieve practically anything.

STEPS TO BEING BRAVE

Make a list of the ten things you most *fear* might happen at your school.

2 BRAVERY IS KEEPING YOUR HEAD WHEN ALL ABOUT YOU ARE LOSING THEIRS

I recently found this quote from a fellow head teacher describing his feelings about his role:

> Sometimes the weight of living in this atmosphere of responsibility, work and weariness seems almost more than I can bear. I feel like a bird in a cage, beating against the bars, longing to be free, but baffled everywhere.

Sound familiar? Have you ever felt like a caged bird? Have you ever beaten against the bars and been 'baffled'? I know such sentiments resonated strongly with me when I first read it. Or what about pushing water uphill? Ever tried that? Or squaring a circle? Or plaiting fog? Tasks like these are nothing when compared to the overriding task we'll look at within the pages of this book – that of being a head teacher in a school in the twenty-first century.

Leading a school is one of the greatest privileges on earth: to stand at the front of a group of highly creative professionals and equally creative – and equally challenging – young people, and be their leader, their representative, the person who can help bring out their best or simply stand in the way of them achieving their potential. This is a role that fills me with awe and respect for every other head teacher who cares about doing his or her job well. It is what makes me not only feel humble each day but also committed to doing my best, day after day.

But, sadly, being a head teacher can be one of the most desperately soul-destroying jobs an educational professional can do. And I say that as a head teacher with eleven years of experience in the role across a variety of different schools, not to mention the fact that I am by various measures a 'successful' head teacher, one who has at least succeeded in steering schools along the desired path. I used to find that my outlook on the role would fluctuate on a weekly basis. There would be good weeks and there would be challenging weeks and then there would be the occasional stinker of a week where you would really ask yourself if you were up to it and, even if you were, was it all worth it anyway? Surely there must be easier jobs out there: brain surgeon maybe, or Chief Inspector of Schools? These days, however, such fluctuations in my job satisfaction occur many times *across the same day*. I can start the day on a high, be on my knees by lunchtime and be back on top of the world by teatime. Or the other way round. A good leader isn't marked out by *not* experiencing such trials and tribulations. That's part of the day job in many ways. The good leader, indeed the great leader, is marked out by the way in which his or her internal roller-coaster of self-doubt, negativity and sheer desperation is rendered invisible to the outside world. What staff, pupils and parents wish to see is the proverbial swan gliding effortlessly across the millpond (OK, in my case, more oil tanker than swan but you get the idea). For me, this is where bravery comes in. In fact, if you want a good working definition, it would be quite simply the individual's ability to maintain high external optimism at times of lowest internal optimism. Nothing to it really.

If you were to chart the rise and fall across a day of the internal optimism levels of a head teacher it would look something, worryingly, like this:

And that's on a good day.

So, whilst all that is going on in the head teacher's internal world, what should the external world look like? This is what people want and, indeed, deserve to see:

Honesty is what you show when the line remains above the midpoint. Bravery is what you show when it dips below. These, then, are the times when the greatest display of bravery is demanded of me:

If every day is whole series of battles to keep yourself going, let alone the rest of the staff and children you profess to be leading, why on earth would any sane thinking individual do the job? Let's address the obvious answer first: the money. Sure enough, pay these days can be very attractive (although not all school heads are on the sort of six-figure salaries that the press like to bandy about). No amount of money, though, can compensate for the destructive effect that the role has on many head teachers' lives. I know, sadly, of some wonderful heads who should have years of educational leadership and transformation left in them, but have been bullied and hit upon to such a level that they can fight the stress no longer. There are heads who don't want to hang up their boots, but are mere shells of the people they used to be. And these are the lucky ones. I can add to this shameful roll-call other colleagues suffering divorce, illness and even early death. For me, personally, the strain hit in an unexpected way when in January 2012 I suffered a small stroke during a meeting in my office at school. Thankfully prompt action, lifelong medication and a better diet mean it may have been a blessing in disguise, but it did remind me what is important in life – and it isn't keeping the latest Secretary of State for Education happy!

So, if the job brings with it so much stress and risk, why do we do it? I guess that one of the first reasons for opting to be a school leader, especially in some of the UK's more challenging educational environments, as I have, is the desire to be a driver of change. The money is good and it serves as some form of compensation, but if you do the job for the salary you will soon realize that it will never be compensation enough for all that you go through. Nor will it ever compete with the feeling you get on those occasions when it all goes right and you see those young people – and their teachers – really shine in ways that you know you have helped make happen. Rather than simply serving as a boost to their bank balance, their pension or their ego, most of the heads I have met are in the job because they feel that they can make a genuine difference where it is needed. Their motivation is good and, in this head's opinion, comes from the right place.

> Most of the heads I have met are in the job because they feel that they can make a genuine difference where it is needed.

But motivation and the moral high ground are not enough. This is where the need for bravery – and lots of it – kicks in.

Let's be clear though. Bravery is not just one single action. It is not having a crisis, dealing with it and then everything returning to a state of calm. You are not a passer-by rescuing a kitten from a burning building, receiving a medal and then going back to the office to count paper clips. In fact, it is relatively easy to act bravely in response to a one-off event. Even if the event isn't just a one off, it can become wearing but it is still manageable. No, what we are talking about with school headship is a metaphorical fire in an allegorical cattery that's sandwiched between a cat food factory and a fish market, where no matter how many animals you retrieve from the figurative flames there are always more just recklessly diving right back in for you to go and rescue again. Bravery in headship is relentless. It is for the long haul. It is the need to show courage day in, day out, month in, month out. It is showing courage when it seems, at times, in your darkest moments, that there is no sign of hope on the horizon, no sign of an end to the journey, when the light at the end of the tunnel has not only been switched off to save energy but the tunnel itself is being bricked up as you travel along it!

So, now that we have that bleak perspective out of the way, the stuff they don't really tell you about at 'how to be a head teacher' school, we are left with one question really – are you brave enough? After all, there is plenty in the history books about brave warriors. There is quite a bit about brave leaders. But there is very little about brave head teachers. How does your experience and understanding of what being brave is all about compare with the quotations below from a variety of people who know a little about the subject? Certainly, as far as I'm concerned, each one of these definitions brings me a little closer to my own understanding of the term:

> I learned that courage was not the absence of fear, but the triumph over it. The brave man is not he who does not feel afraid, but he who conquers the fear.
>
> Nelson Mandela

> The opposite of bravery is not cowardice but conformity.
>
> Robert Anthony

If we take the generally accepted definition of bravery as a quality which knows no fear, I have never seen a brave man. All men are frightened. The more intelligent they are, the more they are frightened.

George S. Patton

The man who knows when not to act is wise. To my mind bravery is forethought.

Euripides

Bravery is the capacity to perform properly even when scared half to death.

Omar N. Bradley

A hero is no braver than an ordinary man, but he is braver five minutes longer.

Ralph Waldo Emerson

The bravest are surely those who have the clearest vision of what is before them, glory and danger alike, and yet notwithstanding, go out and meet it.

Thucydides

Bravery, then, is not about being big and strong. It certainly isn't about being fearless as many people mistakenly think. It is about acting when others won't or not acting when others do. It may be doing things others don't or, if you're doing things others do, doing them for longer. It certainly always seems to be about doing them even when you are scared stiff of what could or probably will happen. Whatever bravery is to you, by definition, it is not an easy thing to pull off. Talking of things that aren't easy to pull off, let me set the scene …

> Bravery is about acting when others won't or not acting when others do. It may be doing things others don't or, if you're doing things others do, doing them for longer.

I am the Principal of Nottingham University Samworth Academy (NUSA). I had been awarded the job after a gruelling series of interviews (in which not all the decision-makers were in favour of my application) that I undertook whilst the head of Serlby Park 3–18 Learning Community. This was a school (which I wrote about in my book, *Are You Dropping the Baton?*) where we had successfully brought together an infant school, a junior school and a secondary school as one genuine through-school. The process of taking three challenging schools and turning them into one successful school was an enormous adventure that required more than its fair share of imagination, good fortune, passion and, of course, bravery. Based in a former pit village on the Nottinghamshire–Yorkshire border, we had utilized the existing buildings of the three schools that were on three different sites. 'Do you want to wait until we have the funds to build a brand new school?' I was asked by the local authority. 'No,' I had replied, 'a school is more than its buildings.' This was a philosophy that would be sorely challenged just a few years later, but one that I'm glad to say I still hold to be true.

Despite the work to be done at Serlby Park, I felt that I needed a new challenge (there is perhaps a fine line between bravery and recklessness) and my eye was soon wandering over the jobs section in the *TES*. I was immediately attracted by the call for a 'Principal Designate' at NUSA for a number of reasons, the most notable of which were:

- It was the country's first academy backed by dual university business sponsorship.

- I would have four terms to help plan the new school during which time I would be based at the university.

- They wished to appoint someone passionate about all-through education.

- The East Midlands was an area I knew and loved (having studied for my degree there, started my teaching there and met and married my wife in the area too).

Much as I didn't want to leave Serlby Park, the pull of NUSA began. I threw my hat into the ring and after a series of demanding rounds I was the only one left. I immediately recognized that the task was immense, but the sponsors were exactly what I had hoped for: supportive, passionate and very people-orientated. Academy sponsors are the people who replace the role of the local authority in guiding the direction of the learning within their academies. Some can be dictatorial and severe, trying to control every breath within the academy; however, Sir David Samworth and the University of Nottingham had very clear views of the transformation they wished me to achieve and were with me every step of the way, always offering their resources to support the journey. What was clear, though, was that they were determined I had the support to do it *my* way. The selection procedure ensured that their ethos and mine matched perfectly. However, a school is also more than its ethos and, before my feet were accustomed to their new position beneath my temporary desk at the university, I was being asked for some flesh and bones to go with the philosophy. For example: What were my plans for the curriculum? The staffing structure? The school's policies? The building management? The pastoral systems? The uniform?

Leadership means not only having answers to these questions but also having the courage to stand by them when they are questioned (for questioned they will be). It also means being prepared to hear these questions and change your mind if you need to, without losing the strength of those original convictions or confidence in yourself. It is a fine line, like everything else in leadership. However, starting with a clean piece of paper when it comes to a new school is a real piece of cake compared to the two greatest challenges facing me.

The first one I knew about: the academy replaced an old school with a poor reputation. The majority of staff, pupils and parents were 'imprinted' with the old habits, beliefs, attitudes and the old way of doing things. At least, I had thought to myself, the brand new building with all its shiny new equipment and facilities would be a great lever to help dispel these old patterns of thinking for good.

Or at least that's what I thought until the second biggest challenge made it itself known, one that came as a surprise to us all: the new building wouldn't be ready until twelve months after we launched the new school. It was like the gods had heard me expounding on the way in which a school is more than its buildings and decided to really put this philosophy to the test. The existing buildings would have been eligible for the title 'most miserable, run down and dilapidated school buildings in the UK' if the word 'buildings' hadn't been too much of an overstatement. They were truly awful. The opportunity for transformation was monumental but so was the scale of the task before us. My bravery levels had to be scaled up considerably to be up to such a task. This is why I feel I am now in a position to write a book such as this.

If I'm being honest (and, interestingly, bravery is about both being brave enough to be truly honest and, at times, lying through your teeth that all will be well) then my last year leading NUSA has been one of the most difficult of my life. Every day seemed like a battle. Every aspect of the job an ordeal. I felt that each step I took was being scrutinized by so many people who were all expecting me to do what, in their minds at least, they thought I should be doing. This, more often than not, boiled down to what everyone else would have done in my circumstances. But I'm afraid I don't work that way. If they had wanted me to lead a school like everyone else would have, then that is who they should have appointed to lead it – everyone else. But as the wise man once said, 'Only dead fish go with the river'.

I can't look my pay cheque in the eye, let alone the children, staff and my own family, if I do things that I know, deep down, are fundamentally, categorically and absolutely the wrong things to do, even if everyone is telling me to do them. Either I do what I feel is the right thing to do or I leave. That is what being a leader is all about. It is that simple. But such simplicity brings with it an almost unbearable pressure and it is in the face of this pressure, which is in many ways of your own making, that you will need to display your greatest levels of bravery.

With so much inner turmoil, the brave leader must show a positive face, an unstinting outward belief that not only is the battle eminently winnable but it is also practically won, all bar the shouting. It is about remembering to look at what you have achieved rather than only seeing the mountain left to climb. It is about keeping your eye on the goal so that you see more than just the obstacles. It is being constantly vigilant to the fact that it is easy to let your internal well-being slip as you start the slide down towards negativity. (Just last year I remember speaking at a conference about leadership and suddenly became conscious that I was on remote control myself, wrapped up in the dilemmas and worries of my own school. On listening to what I was saying I realized that I should take more notice of myself!)

Which brings me back to the quotation at the opening of this chapter, the one in which the head teacher is battling with the weight of all that work and responsibility, and the weariness of it all. Did that describe for you, like it did for me, your own battle with the job?

Maybe you've met this head, although I doubt it. He died in 1887. His name is Edward Thring and he was head teacher at Uppingham School. So, maybe our role hasn't changed as much as we believe, particularly when you read the words of the Canadian educator, imperialist and author, Sir George Robert Parkin (1846–1922) who wrote of Thring;

> He dreamed of breaking through the monotony and the grind of teachers' lives, the treadmill of constant preparation and ceaseless evaluation, which are so apt to dry up and narrow mind and spirit. (Parkin, 1900: 124)

On one hand I find this reassuring – the fact that our troubles are not new and what we feel today countless others have experienced, endured and survived. Yet, I also find it rather worrying, that this battle has been going on for so long and with no end in sight.

So, bravery in the world of educational leadership, we can be sure, is decidedly nothing new. Heads have clearly needed it for centuries. But one thing is for sure, they have never needed it more than they do now.

STEPS TO BEING BRAVE

Look at your list of ten things you fear. Then remember FEAR stands for False Expectations Appear Real. So now remove five that are realistically *not* going to happen.

.

BRAVE
POLITICS

3 BRAVERY IS POINTING OUT HOW PREDICTABLE POLITICS CAN BE

Society in general does not cope well with change. In fact, it often responds in such a way as to oppose the change that is trying to make itself felt. Such resistance, rather than being a process designed by curmudgeons in the pub (or the staffroom) in order to ensure things always remain like they always were, can actually be seen as an extension of a perfectly natural phenomenon – that of dynamic equilibrium. I'm a chemist by training so I know about these things. Trust me. A chemical system will always find its natural balance, or what is known as its 'equilibrium state'. Once it has found this, any further alterations to the system will always be opposed by the system, thus restoring and ensuring the original balance.

Perhaps this could be understood by using a real-life example, one that you should recognize as a staple of any GCSE science paper worth its sodium chloride. If you look at what is known as the Haber process, the chemical reaction where ammonia (the starting point for fertilizers and many other important chemicals) is made from the gases nitrogen and hydrogen, then the reaction is often represented as:

$$\text{Nitrogen} + \text{Hydrogen} \rightleftharpoons \text{Ammonia}$$

Clever little things those chemicals. The ones on the left hand side of the reaction take up more space than the product they make. What happens if you put them in a bigger container? The reaction moves to fill the space by forming less of the smaller product and returning to the bigger reactants on the left. If you put them in a smaller container wondrously we get more of the smaller product (the one on the right). In other words, the reaction always tries to oppose the change you make.

If millions of tiny inanimate molecules can respond in this apparently logical way, it is perhaps not too great a leap of imagination to assume that millions of humans may combine in a similar way. Maybe we could summarize our human dynamic equilibrium as:

$$\text{Tradition} + \text{Rules} \rightleftharpoons \text{Change}$$

What we see, then, is that when change is implemented or imposed on a community, the natural response is for the community to try to resist the change or, as quickly as possible, regain its past position. This is something it does by focusing on traditions and historical successes: 'In the old days …', 'When I was at school …', 'You're not allowed to do that …'

Governments also suffer from this irresistible drive for equilibrium – the current UK government has come to power at a time of great national and international uncertainty, at a time when financial structures and 'trusted' organizations are collapsing around us. It is, therefore, no surprise to find that rather than using this period of upheaval as an opportunity to move forward and discover new innovations to move us on in this new 'reality', instead we find a drive to reintroduce standards and 'the way things were' from a previous 'golden' age. Jumpers for goalposts anyone?

Talking of football, education will always be used as the government's, *any* government's, football. It is one of the front-line services which have shown the ready ability for quick responses and some easy-win headlines. If someone threw up a study revealing an overriding ignorance of the breeding habits of the common warthog you can be assured that Warthog Studies will be a compulsory part of the National Curriculum before the year is out, especially if the incumbent Secretary of State for

Education did a project on warthogs when they were at some leafy grammar school decades earlier.

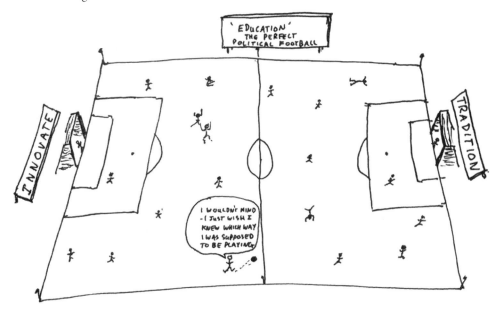

Therefore when faced with a challenge to the equilibrium, governments will respond with whatever tools they have at their disposal to resist the change and restore the balance. Education is one such tool. Whenever some new innovation has been introduced and grasped by the teaching profession, the powers that be will almost instinctively make a 'trad-itional' response, trying to gravitate back to a 'safe' central ground under the 'back to basics' rallying cry so beloved of Middle England.

Put into our formula, it might look something like this:

$$\begin{aligned} &\text{Traditional Curriculum + Traditional Teaching and Learning} \\ &\rightleftharpoons \text{Innovative Curriculum + Innovative Teaching and Learning} \end{aligned}$$

In 2012 we face the greatest uncertainty for a century around financial, political and industrial relations – and, remember, uncertainty and challenge mean an opportunity for innovation and progress. The UK government has responded not by grasping the nettle but by returning to a flawed process: the use of key performance indicators (or KPIs) to drive forward a return to a 1950s model of education. (I'm not sure if you can drive forward going backwards but they seem to have managed it.)

Now, by the time you read this there could be another government in place or you may be reading it in a place with a whole different government anyway. The thing is, whenever and wherever you read this book, if you are a head teacher, your job is to make happen in your school what governments think should happen in all schools. If not, you're out on your ear. Knowing how ridiculous the situation is doesn't help. In fact, it makes it worse. You may believe that the direction the government is sending you in is incorrect. You may even have all the academic and empirical evidence to prove beyond a shadow of a doubt that the government is wrong, not to mention your own proven experience of knowing what a school needs and acting upon that successfully. None of that counts one jot, as you will be measured by the reactionary indicators that prevail. And it is in this gap between what you are told to do and what you know is right where your bravery will be most called upon.

This may be the time to touch on those dreaded key performance indicators so beloved of systems people and governments who forget that the education system isn't actually a system; it is something far more complex than that, what with it being full of people. I refer to KPIs as 'Knowingly Pointless Indicators' and loathe them with a vengeance, not because I don't want my school to excel but because they can have the exact opposite effect if we're not careful. Margaret Wheatley, who has inspired my love of seeking scientific understandings of organizational issues, has produced a superb book that I would recommend to all head teachers entitled *Leadership and the New Science*. In it she suggests that just as it is impossible to specify both the position and energy of an electron (this is Heisenberg's uncertainty principle, but then you knew that), once you measure one output of an organization, you weaken the ability to develop another. I think its correct scientific title is 'taking your eye off the ball'.

> It is in the gap between what you are told to do and what you know is right where your bravery will be most called upon.

Consider what happened a few years back within the UK's National Health Service and the then-government's obsession with targets. Hospitals were told their success would be judged by the length of their waiting lists. A simple strategy and a worthy one. Let's grab some great headlines by cutting the time that voters, I mean patients, have to wait for operations or to see specialists or whatever aspect of the health service it was they had been waiting for. Therefore, one of the performance indicators became the average time it took for a patient arriving in casualty to be seen. And of course, concomitant with KPIs come the inevitable league tables. So, what did such a well-meaning measure achieve? It is no surprise to learn that many hospitals became fixated on moving their way up the league tables. Did this cause them to embark on a deep and wide restructuring of the patient experience? Of course not. Human nature, when driven to perform by external targets and arbitrary measures, will do what human nature always does and find a creative variety of 'tricks' to 'achieve' the KPI.

For example, and we have probably all experienced this, the hospital bosses whose responsibility it is to achieve the KPIs, and not ensure people get better, employ a nurse not to treat patients but to interview every patient within fifteen minutes of their arrival. Suddenly, the queue has magically gone away and the hospital has achieved its KPI. Success! Everyone looks good. Except the overall patient experience, which does not figure as a KPI, has deteriorated. The delight at being seen within a few minutes of arrival evaporates as they go into their second hour of sitting in the now invisible second queue.

That this will happen seems obvious to me. An organization will work to fulfil the performance indicator that will bring it the best and often quickest reward, especially if there is a financial incentive attached to it, as is often the case. And when you're a cash-strapped public service, who would blame you? Hospitals are only human after all. Like schools. It is not the people to blame here but a system that works only on paper and fails to remember that it is living, breathing human beings who actually have to try to make the system work. KPIs drive organizations to achieve KPIs. That is all. And I am yet to find a single KPI that, on its own, drives whole-scale organizational change.

In fact, let's put this claim to the test …

4 BRAVERY IS REMEMBERING HOW STUPID THE SYSTEM CAN BE

Here's a little task I have put together to show exactly how key performance indicators don't work. Or, more accurately, how they work in such a way as to make the whole situation worse.

Let's imagine the government is in charge of family counselling. The answer to all successful improvements in any system, as every government knows, is to create a series of KPIs. And, with a family just being a simple 'domestic system', such an approach is bound to work here too. This is my patented six-step KPI-driven approach to complete domestic system harmony optimization:

1   The first step is to list the top ten things that annoy you about the behaviour of your children/partner/parents. Try and limit it to ten!

2   Then look at the behaviour that is number one on your list of pet peeves and design an appropriate 'punishment and reward' scheme that will serve to diminish that behaviour.

3   Apply the scheme for one week.

4   At the end of the week, has that number one most disliked behaviour diminished? If no, go back to step two and come up with a juicier carrot or a bigger stick. If yes, go to step five.

5   Has there been any change in the other nine behaviours that were on your list, the ones for which you didn't have a punishment or reward scheme?

6   Overall, taking into account the full extent of all ten behaviours that annoy you most about your family members, have they become any less annoying?

If you have followed this process through and found that everyone is now getting on so much better as a family unit, then I'm clearly in the wrong job and shall go and volunteer for Relate. If, however, as I suspect may be more the case, you were to find an improvement in annoying habit number one but deterioration in some of the other items on the list, then you will certainly have got my point about the nature of KPIs. What's more, you may well now have a situation where you have discovered new things to be annoyed about as result of the KPI exercise: 'Yes dear, I know I said that chewing your food with your mouth open was the most annoying thing about you but liquidizing everything before you eat it isn't exactly what I had in mind! Another glass of pie?'

5 BRAVERY IS ACCEPTING SLIGHTLY LESS THAN PERFECTION

'This isn't good enough!' cries the politician.

'We need to set a tough KPI!' is the response.

In 'real' life, developing successful relationships is all about employing a plethora of small steps to move us forward and closer together. We praise and subtly reward actions we desire, often mirroring them ourselves, and together grow and develop. We soon learn that 'nagging' about a number of undesirable behaviours isn't good for us and doesn't do much to change the behaviours either.

Sadly, these 'common sense' lessons from real life are not used in the system-driven world of education. Here the overemphasis on the achievement of pupils at age 16 (at secondary level) and at the end of Key Stage 2 (at primary level), merely serves to act as the tail wagging the dog.

Let us look at the evidence.

'WE MUST RAISE STANDARDS' KPI NUMBER ONE:

Schools were told that they will be placed in a league table based on the percentage of pupils achieving five or more GCSEs at Grade C or above.

HOW DID SOME SCHOOLS RESPOND?

There was a development of new, mainly coursework-based qualifications that allowed many pupils to achieve four GCSE equivalents from one subject alone.

WHICH HAD THE FOLLOWING RESULTS:

The schools that put their students through these new qualifications moved up the league tables at an impressive rate, receiving plaudits all round. In a number of cases, head teachers were rewarded for their contribution to the 'improvement of educational outcomes' with a special mention in the New Year Honours list.

SO WHAT HAPPENED NEXT?

Most schools then realized they too needed to embrace the new qualifications in order to fight for their position in the league tables. They dutifully shifted their curriculum appropriately. Furthermore, many organizations recognized that there is a profit to be made in these new awards and a plethora of alternatives appeared. Most schools successfully introduced new subjects, each worth a handful of GCSEs.

RESULTING IN:

Politicians started to worry that their attempt to raise educational standards may have had the, er, opposite effect. While schools were being 'rewarded' for 'improved outcomes' (number of pupils leaving schools with five or more GCSEs and/or equivalents) curriculum time and focus on traditional subjects decreased. Businesses complained that school-leavers were deficient in core skills. Some of the more 'unusual' courses (NVQ in Cake Decorating being a classic example) became a focus for media doubts regarding the rigour of these qualifications. Newspapers led the 'standards are falling' battle cry.

THEREFORE:

'This isn't good enough!' cries the politician.

'We need a new KPI!' is the response.

'WE MUST RAISE STANDARDS' KPI NUMBER TWO:

Schools were told they will be put in a new improved league table based on the percentage of their pupils who achieve five A–C grades at GCSE including English and Maths.

HOW DID SOME SCHOOLS RESPOND?

Many schools immediately replaced sections of their 'additional GCSEs' and refocused their curriculum on the 'core' subjects. Schools which had not followed the mass dive into the alternative curriculum pool smugly found themselves climbing back up the popularity tables (although whether this was from foresight or indolence can only be judged on a case-by-case basis).

WHICH HAD THE FOLLOWING RESULTS:

Many teachers who had immersed themselves in these new qualifications and had successfully, yet now pointlessly, dealt with the huge workload associated with such tasks became disillusioned, their work devalued almost before it had begun. A cynicism seemed to spread amongst sections of the profession, with English and Maths departments becoming the primary focus of school life, advantaged not just in contact time but also in the lifeblood of school life – their share of capitation!

SO WHAT HAPPENED NEXT?

Schools became very imaginative in ways to maximize their English and Maths results: battles emerged to find the 'easiest' examination boards and pupils were entered for multiple sittings of each paper, being allowed as many bites of the cherry as possible. Highly paid consultants (many of whom were government approved) began circulating schools selling their wares and theories to the highest bidders. Success in English and Maths exams increased at a faster level than any other subject.

RESULTING IN:

Politicians began to worry that the improvement in examination results was not being matched by a transformation in the actual essential skills of literacy and numeracy. There was an impression of a decline in standards, and a political desire for a move to the type of education epitomized by 1950s grammar schools. Newspapers led the 'standards are falling' battle cry.

THEREFORE:

'This isn't good enough!' cried the politician.

'We need a new KPI!' is the response.

'WE MUST RAISE STANDARDS' KPI NUMBER THREE:

Schools were told that they will be placed in a new, new improved league table based on the performance of their pupils in the English Baccalaureate (not to be confused with the International Baccalaureate which is a diverse, rigorous, post-16 qualification recognized around the world that takes into account creativity, thinking skills and social commitment as well as independent academic study. No, not to be confused at all …). This EBacc would include only the 'important subjects': Maths, English, Science, a Humanities and a Modern Foreign Language (not to be confused with the core curriculum of a 1950s grammar school which took into account only the 'important subjects': Maths, English, Science, a Humanities and a Modern Foreign Language. Oh, hang on a minute …). To guarantee that genuine 1950s grammar school feel to the examination system, coursework would be significantly cut back and only the pupils' first sitting of the exam will count. This ensures that education serves to exclude and divide rather than offer something for all young people in a caring, inclusive way. Welcome back to the good old days …

HOW DID SOME SCHOOLS RESPOND?

Panic ensued. Many schools had only recently replaced their languages teachers in the drive to meet the first KPI (the then-government had kindly assisted at that point by removing the legal requirement to teach languages beyond the age of 14). The teaching of Humanities as an integrated subject had also been encouraged, which almost inevitably reduced the number of students wishing to study History and Geography.

WHICH HAD THE FOLLOWING RESULTS:

Schools quickly ditched vocational/alternative qualifications, no matter how successful they were in providing an inclusive education for all their children. The curriculum is being rewritten almost as it is being delivered and pupils are being crammed into 'short-course' Humanities and Languages at an alarming rate. The fact, overlooked by anyone in a position of power in the education system with no direct experience of education (i.e. everyone in a position of power in the Department for Education) is that a curriculum needs a minimum of three years to design and implement – so to announce these rule changes with less than eighteen months notice is analogous to completely changing the rules of a football match just after half-time.

SO WHAT HAPPENED NEXT?

Most schools are repositioning their curriculum and staffing faster than a chameleon changes its colours, whilst the government is changing its position as fast as a leopard changes its spots. More creative (i.e. none-core) subjects are having their time and capitation slashed as schools attempt to ensure they are not left languishing at the bottom of the latest version of the new, new improved league tables. The students who are managing to cope with a traditional academic setting are doing well in a traditional academic way but will be in for a shock when they reach the twenty-first century world of work, and many other children are at risk of becoming school failures again.

RESULTING IN:

It is almost inevitable that a shrinking of the curriculum has already begun, mainly evident in a reduction of creative elements. The concept of the 'well-rounded pupil' has been discarded in place of the 'EBacc pupil'. I don't imagine it will be long before someone is complaining about the lack of technological or artistic talent being produced by our schools, although no doubt certain newspapers will still be leading the 'standards are falling' battle cry.

So how long before …?

'This isn't good enough!' cries the politician.

'We need a new KPI!' is the response.

Is it any surprise that I often refer to KPIs as 'the devil's work'?

STEPS TO BEING BRAVE

Write a set of 'real performance indicators' that you would like to be used for your school.

6 BRAVERY IS HAVING THE STRENGTH TO SEE KPIS FOR WHAT THEY ARE

Go back to the equilibrium equation I mentioned earlier in this section:

$$\text{Traditional Curriculum + Traditional Teaching and Learning} \\ \rightleftharpoons \text{Innovative Curriculum + Innovative Teaching and Learning}$$

It is a simple task to predict that once the shift to a more traditional curriculum is completed, some bright [*sic*] new politician is going to proclaim that teachers have lost their way, and introduce a drive for more innovation.

As a leader your job isn't to do what is asked of you at the expense of the people in your care. Your job is to whatever you need to for the people in your care, and that includes often resisting doing what you are supposed to do.

And that's why people need you to be brave.

STEPS TO BEING BRAVE

Award a 'Brave Teacher' prize to one of your staff who has shown courage and initiative.

7 BRAVERY IS NOT ALWAYS DANCING TO THE POLITICAL TUNE

Dealing with the national educational and political landscape is one thing as a head teacher, but what about when it is closer to home? The newly appointed, informed and brave leader is immediately faced with a dilemma: you may actually agree with the political view that the current educational standards in your school area are not acceptable. Years of failure, where the only success students achieve is in hitting the low expectations dished up to them, should not be tolerated and cannot go on. However, you may well disagree with the method(s) by which change is being forced upon the community.

The *informed leader* – and I use and reuse that term deliberately – has an idea of what they think is the best way by which the local community can be helped to help itself. The trouble is that this carefully and diplomatically gleaned local intelligence may well be at odds with what the external monitor (in my case the Department for Education) deems to be the way forward for the school. What's more, political timescales are almost always out of sync with those required for effecting lasting change. The brave head does all that he or she can to resist the quick-win merchants who are involved in your project, your community and your people, just long enough to secure their next promotion, knighthood or election. And there's plenty of those around, ready to use you as a rung on their own personal career ladder. Having dealings with them is one thing – inevitable, frustrating and dissatisfying – but learning how to deal with them effectively is something else altogether.

STEPS TO BEING BRAVE

Contact your local MP with a list of five
things because of which he/she should
be proud of your school.

8 BRAVERY IS HAVING THE STRENGTH TO DO THINGS YOUR WAY BECAUSE DEEP DOWN YOU KNOW YOUR WAY IS THE RIGHT WAY

When I was appointed to my role at Nottingham University Samworth
Academy, I was subjected to many rounds of interrogation and intel-
lectual challenge to prove I was up to the job (two whole days of
interviews including a staff interview, a pupil interview, four panel interviews, a presentation, three hours of psychometric testing, an hour-long
one-to-one with Sir David Samworth and a final interview to a panel of
ten including a senior Department for Education representative). For
me, the most painful part of the process was fielding questions from that
high profile DfE member of the panel who didn't like my long-term
view of change. 'We want community transformation and we want it
now' was his mantra. I too, of course, wanted change – in fact it was my
core purpose – but we differed greatly in our opinion regarding the
speed with which we expected long-term sustainable change to be
achieved. He believed that change should be made by whatever super-
ficial, headline grabbing, ill thought-through, short-term action possible,

even if this included employing strategies and policies that might, in the end, actually serve to limit achievement. Personally, I was not prepared to make short-term, quick-win promises in lieu of long-term, long-lasting change. Put simply, I knew I had to make a difference because my career depended on it. He needed to make a difference because his post depended on it.

In the end, this individual was the only person on the selection panel who was dead set against me being offered the post. I am pleased at both a personal and professional level to have been offered the opportunity to be proving him wrong.

STEPS TO BEING BRAVE

Make a presentation to your governors comparing what you want from your school with what the government seem to want.

BRAVE
CURRICULUM

9 BRAVERY IS GIVING TEACHERS THE SPACE TO ENCOURAGE GENIUS

The current drive to envelop young people in a narrow one-size-fits-all blanket of traditional academic subjects may well mean that we, in education, are tempted to take our eye off the ball when it comes to the development of broader work and life skills. At the time of writing, the current Secretary of State for Education, Michael Gove, has just announced a new English Baccalaureate with the dire warning, according to a report in *The Guardian*, that 'a sizeable proportion of students would leave school with no qualifications' (Watt, 2012). At a time when we desperately need young people skilled in enterprise, innovation and adaptability, the system may well be serving to squash those very skills in an attempt to meet its spurious 'traditional' goals. As Doman and Doman say, genius is not about the innate intelligence of a child but about how much fun they consider learning to be (2005: 82).

STEPS TO BEING BRAVE

Ask your staff to nominate pupils for 'Genius of the Week' awards. Collate a book of your school's geniuses (or is it genii?).

10 BRAVERY IS HAVING THE COURAGE TO HAVE FUN – AND EXPECTING YOUR STAFF TO DO THE SAME

Here's a simple question to help you arrive at a much overlooked truth. How much do you remember from your own schooling? Is it (a) that lesson where we copied a diagram about photosynthesis, or (b) the time we all acted out the carbon cycle and the teacher nearly broke his ankle impersonating carbon dioxide? (Clue: The answer isn't (a).)

Many teachers are susceptible to a destructive disease: 'Wemustimpartforyoutolearn-itus'. In some schools it is endemic. The symptoms of this malady include:

- A propensity to talk too much in lessons.

- A tendency to believe that to miss the next lesson would severely hamper a pupil's education.

- An inflated view of the importance of their particular subject area.

- An inflated view of the importance of learning the next curriculum objective related to their subject area.

- A delusional fancy that their key function is to impart subject knowledge to the masses.

- A misguided belief that they are teaching subjects not children.

- An associated belief that the whole child is, therefore, someone else's responsibility.

What I am *not* saying is that classroom-based factual input is unimportant. It is, after all, a key part of the foundation on which students can build their learning. But firstly, there are ways of children acquiring facts in the classroom that don't have to involve the teacher talking them into children's heads, and secondly, if this is our main tool for delivery we are in danger of losing huge sections of the current generation of learners. So, the brave head is the one practically forcing the staff to introduce an element of fun into the serious business of learning and who models this by introducing fun into the serious business of running a school. In doing so, in making day-to-day life at the school enjoyable for all, you also make it memorable. Bravery one; mediocrity nil!

STEPS TO BEING BRAVE

Have a theme for your learning walks within your school. Make it clear you are hoping to see examples of learning being made fun.

11 BRAVERY IS ENCOURAGING YOUR STAFF TO LET GO OF THE BELIEF THAT THEIR SUBJECT IS THE MOST IMPORTANT THING IN A CHILD'S LIFE

Whilst I understand the despair of teachers who have conscientiously prepared their lesson only to find half the class involved in another subject's field trip/theatre group/study visit, it would be wrong on so many levels to deny children these opportunities. When faced with a potential conflict situation, I often remind staff of the lesson I learnt whilst carrying out a research project for my MA in European Education. I had the good fortune to be given the task of studying the effects of a transnational student exchange programme. The European Secondary School Student Exchange (ESSSE) programme allowed 16-year-old students to swap schools and, indeed, lives with someone from a non-adjacent European country (the 'non-adjacent' bit is important – you've seen the way the scoring works in the Eurovision Song Contest). Instead of beginning their post-16 studies in their own school, the young person ups sticks and moves to the home and school of a similar-aged pupil elsewhere on the Continent. Some of these young people were put in what was, for them, seemingly intolerable situations (for example, in the absence of any common language one Portuguese youth had to use broken English as the only means of communication in a Latvian household). For a number of the participants, the educational experience was even worse, when they were placed in a school that did not teach the subject for which the student was wishing to specialize (such as the Croatian girl interested in becoming a designer who was placed in a science-only school in Estonia).

In the middle of this mass of poor international administration, my role was to evaluate the educational impact of these experiences on the youngsters. Would this three-month distraction at a key point in a young person's life provide a long-lasting academic, personal and professional benefit or simply, as I feared, put them at a permanent educational disadvantage? My worries were unfounded. Of the 300 young people who entered the programme over the three years, I could find not a single one who had not benefited from the experience. Upon returning to their homes and going back to their own schools, the typical story of reintegration, revealed by project diaries, interviews and questionnaires, could best be summarized as follows:

- **December – return to home and home school**: Despair! 'What have I done?', 'I feel different to all my other classmates', 'I've missed so much', 'I will never catch up'.

- **End of February**: Many had already caught up with 'missed' topics. The majority were already performing in line with their original potential. 'I feel more motivated than my classmates', 'I don't know what they have been doing for the three months I was away – they appear to have stood still'.

- **End of the first year back – summer exams**: Many outperformed all other pupils in their class, most producing higher grades than they were predicted at the start of the course. When asked why they thought this was, the answers included: 'I grew up', 'I decided what was important in life', 'I understood what I wanted from life'.

Many of these pupils had missed about 20% of their taught course and had been placed in an environment that was, in many cases, practically stimulus free, yet they still outperformed their classmates on their return. Or, to put it another way, the students were more successful after having been locked in a metaphorical 'dark cupboard' for three months than they would have been if they had attended every one of their teachers' lessons.

And yet you complain that missing a single one of your periods spells the end of any hope of their academic success ...

STEPS TO BEING BRAVE

Ask your staff to list three things they have taught this week which will have changed a pupil's life.

BRAVE
CHOICES

12 BRAVERY IS KEEPING YOUR EYE ON THE MARATHON WHILST YOU ARE PERFORMING THE SPRINT

Anyone who knows me is aware that I am a lover of analogies (and ties). From chemistry to gardening I love to paint pictures to get my point across. I learned a long time ago that a leader is someone who creates pictures in people's heads, believable, attractive pictures of things being better. Metaphors, analogies and stories all help to get the team on side and moving in the right direction. But of all the metaphors I have ever used the one regarding the marathon and the sprint has been the most telling.

In a nutshell, all the activities engaged in by a school community can be boiled down to two main headings: *marathon* activities – those that are undertaken for long-term benefits and for the greater good of the community as a whole, and *sprint* activities – those that are undertaken for quick wins (often under pressure from external agencies who have the power to sack you if you don't join in that particular race).

> Brave leadership is about ensuring we never lose sight of the marathon.

My time at Nottingham University Samworth Academy has been spent understanding which one was which and ensuring our time was spread between the two in an appropriate way. After all, whilst winning the sprints and keeping our lords and masters off our backs is important, brave leadership is about ensuring we never lose sight of the marathon.

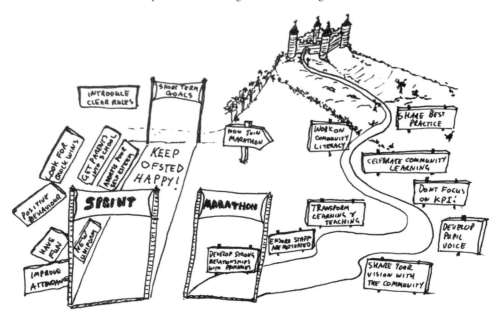

FIVE SPRINT ACTIVITIES

Our first sprint items were all the sort of high-profile alterations that you make to show the community – and your political masters – that things are going to change round here:

- *A new school name.* If possible link to something aspirational recognized by the community. Avoid too close a link with the previous identity. (This is straight out of the Windscale book of management!)

- *A new identity and brand.* Even though I doubted the expenditure at the time, the professional branding of the new academy has reaped many benefits. We chose a strong tree image signifying growth and strength, not to mention the tree of knowledge, which has been used by pupils and staff in a myriad of ways from school brochures to cake stands.

- *A new uniform.* We used a pupil panel to help us and, in partnership with the marketing company, we developed a strong, striking image. One pupil said as he put on the blazer, 'It makes me want to stand up tall and put my shoulders back' (I knew we shouldn't have made it so heavy!). Pupils are easily identified in town and this has led to many more positive reports than negative ones. The local librarian immediately reported an improvement in behaviour, which she attributed to the uniform. I can find little evidence that a uniform alone transforms behaviour but it is an important signal of change, and who am I to argue with a happy librarian?

- *Changes to the building.* As I have already mentioned, the shiny new building we were promised was no more than a building site on day one of NUSA. What we had was a series of terrible, 1950s buildings with weeds growing in the stairwells and an all-pervading sense of hopelessness oozing with the damp through the walls. Even if you are not able to begin in a new building, it is vital you make cosmetic changes to the old one and you make them fast. We ripped out the barriers at reception that had made the place incredibly unwelcoming for students and visitors alike, placed a huge banner over the door and repainted the darkest, dingiest corners in the brightest colours. Our approach was to consider the building like a stage set. It was simply a backdrop to some incredibly uplifting piece of drama and not, ever, the background to a tragedy!

> Self-similarity is not achieved through an exhaustive set of rules but by a few simple principles adhered to by all.

- *Develop a positive behaviour policy.* Pupils actually like rules and guidelines if implemented in what they see as a fair way. Simply swamping a new school with 103 new rules in order to 'make your mark' will only serve to alienate and confuse, as well as use up your paper budget quite quickly. What you are looking to achieve is what Margaret Wheatley talks about when she says, 'Self-similarity is not achieved through an exhaustive set of rules but by a few simple principles adhered to by all' (2006: 148). In other words you don't get people to act in similar ways by giving them step-by-step guides on how to operate within your organization. Rather, you do it by making sure they understand exactly what you are trying to do. It is *similarity in thinking* rather than action that becomes your most important goal. You will never develop a rule for every eventuality so don't try ('Mr Harris, there is a duck in the music room. And it's angry!'). Focus on a few key areas (school uniform is a good example) and draw your lines in the sand. Stating a rule, explaining what will happen if it is broken and then implementing it relentlessly is vital. Just as 'good parent' guides explain that years of battles around bedtime can be avoided by being consistent and clear as early as possible, the same is true with pupil behaviour. Looking back, you could sum up my five essential school rules as:

1   If it isn't going to benefit the pupils' learning, don't do it.

2   If it can be done in a fun way, then why not do it that way.

3   When someone succeeds, share and celebrate it.

4   The glass is half full. Always.

5   If you wouldn't want a visitor to see it – don't do it!

Simple really.

SO WHAT ABOUT THE MARATHON?

Marathon activities are those that neither answer the questions in front of you in the quickest manner possible, nor do they necessarily answer them in the most direct way. To mix my sporting metaphors, it's the swerve ball. For example, if a community has a low level of literacy, the marathon activities are those that set out to address that problem without directly mentioning literacy. That's what they would be expecting! Instead, you run coffee mornings and cookery classes. You organize trips (e.g. Race for Life events, the Harlem Globetrotters in New York, Silverstone racing circuit, Morocco, Snowdon, the Lake District, France, plus numerous theatre trips – to name a few off the top of my head). You lay on clubs (e.g. model helicopters/cars, chess, table tennis, football, pottery, journalism, German, sewing). In fact we made a promise that we would support any club. (It had to be legal though: the first rule of Sewing Club – don't talk about Sewing Club.) In other words, we would support or arrange anything that would serve to develop self-esteem and a new-found enthusiasm for learning. After all, to catch a monkey sometimes you have to look like you are going fishing.

The activities I mention above are the most obvious marathon-type activities. Anyone can run a trip to New York or set up a chess club.

Where the fun starts is when you begin to look at ideas that have never been done before. This is where the bravery really starts to take hold. As I share with you some of these braver marathon activities, the ones of which I am most proud, please remember that they are our ideas, not yours. The rule for marathon planning is that the work should be particular to you and your community, not a copy of activities that have worked elsewhere. Every community has its own character and interests and these must be the starting point for your work as a brave – and informed – head.

STEPS TO BEING BRAVE

In a meeting ask your staff to divide the school's development plan into 'sprint' or 'marathon' activities.

13 BRAVERY IS NOT ALWAYS BEING SERIOUS AT TIMES OF GREAT IMPORTANCE

MARATHON ACTIVITY NUMBER ONE: A TRILOGY OF COMMUNITY PLAYS

What a new school needs to get it off to a good start is a highly innovative and disruptive theatrical experience. In fact, the only thing better than that is to hold three of them. That's the last thing the community would expect. So this is exactly what we laid on, with the support of Nottingham University and a couple of local playwrights.

Part 1 of the trilogy took place over a year before NUSA started in the old building. 'The Road to Bilborough' was a play that focused on the recent history of the area, mixing video excerpts with live action and telling a semi-fictional, humorous story of the area in a Pathé News style. It wove a story around a fictitious family (the Bilboroughs) including video diary entries and local community groups appearing on film. This had the double advantage of involving people who would never consider appearing on a stage as well as capturing the thoughts of a community. We were told that a community such as ours 'would be unlikely to attend plays' but five different venues were used in the neighbourhood and every evening each one was packed out. So there!

Part 2 was entitled 'The Last Inspector' and was performed on the evening that the old school closed – still two months before we opened the doors of the new school in its freshly tarted-up old building. It took an amusing trip through the history of the old school and, again, combined film with live theatre. This piece also enjoyed the benefit of a time machine which allowed the audience to celebrate a number of key events from the past (like the amalgamation with another local school, reliving some of the old characters from the community and even some footage from a twenty-five-year-old sports day). The subtext, however, was very much about something exciting coming just round the corner. The play finished with graphics of the new school and the first public outing for my unofficial school motto:

Aim for the sky and you will hit the ceiling; aim for the ceiling and you will fall flat on your bum.

It may not be Shakespeare but I'm sure if we could fit 'Finis caelum et vos ledo laquearia; finis laquearia et vos cadunt super asinum' onto the school crest we would probably get away with it!

The purpose of this event was not to raise publicity for the new school nor was it to tell the local people how bad everything had been before they were lucky enough to have us – the sponsors, the university, the new leadership – arrive to rescue their 'doomed community'. Rather, it was the subtle, affectionate and purposeful drawing of a line under the past. For better and for worse that was then. And now something different was coming. The message, put across almost subliminally, was of a bright future combined with a sense of fun and excitement, and it played a key role in building new levels of that all-important emotion so critical for all significant change – hope.

The final instalment was held on the Saturday evening after the opening of the new academy building. 'The Future is Now' was the most ambitious of the three plays and was performed al fresco in the plaza in front of the spacious school reception area on a hi-tech stage. (The words 'al fresco', 'plaza', 'hi-tech' and 'spacious' reception area, underline, I think, how far we had come from those awful old school buildings.) On this occasion, rather than being set in the present with time-travelling into the past, it was set in the present but with time-travelling into the future. See what we did there!

I opened the event with the sort of welcoming speech a new head teacher would be expected to give at the opening of a new school building, but my message soon went from fact to fiction as I introduced a time-traveller who brought news of trouble in the future for our community. Through a series of news clips and transmissions 'from the future' (the local old-age-pensioner group in space-age transporters being a particular gem) the story unfolded to the amazement and unreserved enthusiasm of the audience.

As part of the event, the spectators, who numbered almost 1,000, wandered around the new building witnessing experiments of the future – turning cabbages into electricity and curing the common cold to name but two. The culmination of the evening involved the audience joining together to save the academy from some future threat – the clear message being that some amazing things are going to happen over the next fifty years because of this new school opening now.

Would this have been the case if we had held the typical set of introductory getting-to-know-you-here-is-our-new-school-vision-help-yourself-to-a-biscuit-and-a-new-prospectus-on-the-way-out meetings?

STEPS TO BEING BRAVE

Ask the community to submit stories of the area surrounding the school. Collate a book of these stories and hold a book launch.

14 BRAVERY IS NOT CHANGING THINGS, AT LEAST SOME OF THE TIME

MARATHON ACTIVITY NUMBER TWO: THE ACADEMY'S OWN RECORD LABEL

Sometimes when you're implementing major changes, it is the things you don't change that can make all the difference. This was the case for at least one aspect of the work of the predecessor school, not generally noted for its innovation or enthusiasm – namely its own record label. Through this medium young people had been encouraged to demonstrate and develop their talents in singing and performing, and for those involved it had become a real tool for ensuring high levels of engagement in education as a whole.

When creating a new school there can be a temptation to discard all remnants of the old way, but this can be dangerous. Whilst it is important to signal that there are significant systemic changes taking place, I believe it is essential to allow the successful aspects of the past to grow and blossom, using the new regime as an opportunity help these activities grow even further than before (and I will come back to these gardening metaphors later as they are incredibly important). Not only does this ensure that the students – and the school community as a whole – understand that their past is not being disrespected, it also throws up a valuable opportunity for success under the banner of 'marathon activity'.

> It is essential to allow the successful aspects of the past to grow and blossom.

The record label was something we actively supported right from the off, even ensuring that for the first six months it kept its old name, Sharp Records. Our first NUSA Christmas card included a CD of Christmas songs recorded by the pupils on this label and, over time, having the courage to not change things has led to many important benefits for all of us. Most recently, it has had a bit of a re-launch with a new focus on supporting the curriculum and the decision was taken, by all involved, to change its name to NU Start. It is now supported in curriculum time through a Key Stage 4 music business qualification. This allows pupils to manage the label whilst carrying out the formal examination course. Projects have included writing and recording an anti-drugs single which helped launch a city-wide PSHE project and a single, written as part of the Religious Education curriculum and performed by a pupil and member of staff, which reached the top ten in the UK Christian chart and the top twenty in the European one.

However, the project with the most influence for change arose out of the transition work described above. Nottingham University has links with the Mamelodi Trust, a charity dedicated to improving the education and livelihood of people in the South African township of Mamelodi. The trust was looking for ways to raise its profile and the university suggested that the board approach NUSA pupils on the music business course to investigate the possibility of producing a charity single. The pupils met the founders of the charity and were given background information on the issues and the solutions the trust was trying to provide. Pupils then went away, wrote the lyrics and the music and worked on the recording of a single entitled 'Sing, Sing for Africa'.

When the charity officials were first presented with the finished out-come they were literally lost for words and visibly moved. Since then, the single has helped to raise almost £10,000 and has provoked interest in the local press and on TV, not to mention the fact that the two 15-year-old writers and producers were awarded the Nottinghamshire Young People of the Year award in 2011. The biggest thrill for the students involved, though, is that their music is now extremely popular in Mamelodi itself, as you will see if you take a look at the video students from here and there put together to go with the track.[1]

This project, growing out of the achievements of the old school, has had many positive offshoots for the new academy, for our children and for the community as a whole. It has given our students the chance to work at a professional level with adults across the world and to show them – and more importantly themselves – that they can produce work of the very highest standard. It has helped our community recognize that this almost forgotten and certainly neglected corner of Nottingham has the potential to have a positive effect way beyond its boundaries.

And bravery? You may feel you are expected to wipe the slate clean when you take over a new school – to erase the memories of all the practices and leadership that went on before. This is not the brave route. Recognizing that the school had many strengths before you were on the scene, that you are not the only person in the building with a good idea and showing that you are not afraid to continue and celebrate with someone else's good idea – that's where bravery lies.

---

1   You'll find the video featuring NUSA students, teachers and parents, children from our feeder primary schools and young people and teachers from Mamelodi on the NUSA website – www.nusa.org.uk. But watch out, you'll be humming it all day!

STEPS TO BEING BRAVE

Identify the best thing achieved by the school in the last five years. Decide how you are going to repeat this success, but next time, even better.

15 BRAVERY IS NOT MAKING TRANSITION TO THE NEW SCHOOL ALL ABOUT THE NEW SCHOOL

MARATHON ACTIVITY NUMBER THREE: TRANSITION ACTIVITIES THAT CHANGE THE WORLD

Successful transition between primary and secondary education has been a topic of much interest to me. Professor David Hargreaves stated just a few years ago that it was the single biggest issue threatening our education system. It is a national calamity that so many youngsters are still being adversely effected by poor transition, by being thrown into a quick, one-size-fits-all process that fails to recognize the size of the change occurring to these young people at such a delicate stage of their development.

It was my conviction of the need for work in this area that led me to become involved in the formation of Serlby Park (a 3–18 Learning Community) which brought together infant, junior and secondary schools. Of all the many lessons I acquired during this time, the three most important were learning never to underestimate the immense skills residing in our primary schools, never to take any aspect of teaching and learning for granted and, most of all, remembering we should be having more fun in our learning.[2]

So, bearing all this in mind, I was determined not to allow transition to be crammed into a one-day visit to the new school and was therefore delighted when our Nottingham University co-sponsor agreed with me and volunteered to play a key role in our primary transition process. This delight was, I must admit, matched by a high degree of surprise. I might have expected the university to take an interest in transitions at Key Stage 5 but the interest they showed in the younger children was an indication of their genuine commitment to long-term community regeneration. I recommend you go and seek out this expertise for yourselves from whatever university is local to you.

Universities know that lasting change takes time and that an investment mindset is needed. It is not a sprint. This thoughtful and long-term approach is a welcome breath of fresh air after the 'Don't worry about that, it's ages away yet' attitude that tends to prevail in the school sector. 'Why plan ahead today when you can firefight tomorrow?' seems to be our motto. University mechanisms require a much more considered approach to any task or commitment and, with this influence, planning takes place for the next year's intake even before the current intake has taken up its new places.

---

2   For more on this adventure please read *Are You Dropping the Baton?* (2008).

For example, all of our potential feeder primary schools are visited frequently and encouraged to work in the new academy building regardless of whether the pupils involved intend to come to NUSA. After all, this is not about us; it's about the community. Projects have varied from making bugs to Second World War cookery, theatre productions and practical sessions on healthy eating. The culmination of each year's activities is a series of three days focused not just on getting to know the academy but on wider themes. One project was based around the university's link with the township of Mamelodi in South Africa. Primary pupils have worked with teachers who visit Mamelodi (consisting of a team of teachers from NUSA, some primary school teachers and student teachers from the university itself) and also with teachers from the township itself. Artwork and messages are shared between the communities and a grand finale is planned for a day at the university campus for all potential Year 7 children. The day at the campus is not a stuffy 'this is what a university does' day, but instead one of creativity and excitement culminating in a march through the heart of the campus banging drums, chanting and blowing vuvuzalas.

What's more, family members of the children are encouraged to join the procession, many of whom are effectively unaware of the university on their doorstep. With its walled grounds, security guards and barriers, the university can be something they travel around, not venture into. It is somewhere other people go, not them. By inviting family members along we have immediately started to challenge stereotypes and preconceptions – another vital step in the long-term regeneration process of a community. What's more, to hear our young people declare proudly, 'We've been to university', and know that they associate this with having a great time can only be a good thing.

So what does this tell us about bravery? Be prepared to engage with any partners in as wide a way as possible – people will 'expect' certain things of any relationship you form, be it with another educational institution or with a company. The bravery is not in forming these links, but in the enthusiasm and depth of the relationship and in the activities you then put together collaboratively. The most exciting relationships are often the ones that are focused away from the core business of the partner. Keep your mind open to the fact that the most productive partnership with a nuclear physicist may actually be through the fact that they are a champion basket weaver!

> Be prepared to engage with any partners in as wide a way as possible.

STEPS TO BEING BRAVE

Hold a meeting between primary and secondary teachers where conversations about levels are banned. The only topic of conversation allowed is the planning of a joint project.

16 BRAVERY IS HAVING JOBS, ROOMS AND PEOPLE THAT NO ONE ELSE DOES

MARATHON ACTIVITY NUMBER FOUR: EMPLOYING THE WORLD'S FIRST 'AGENT OF WONDER'

The predecessor school had a particularly poor reputation and pupils piled out into the community at the end of each school day without any thought for their studies until the following day. If there was a parent to be seen in the old school it was because they had been summoned there to talk about their child's behaviour. It was never to have a positive conversation about learning. In fact, if I were to be held over a barrel and forced to accept at least one KPI (see Chapters 3–5) it would be one that served to increase the number of ways that a parent can engage with school positively.

It was clear that what I needed was a tall, charismatic lichen expert and magician working on his second PhD whom I could task with the job of bringing the whole community into the school in a positive way and improve GCSE results at the same time. This is where the world's first Agent of Wonder came in.

When appointed as Principal Designate of the new academy, I was lucky and privileged to have time based at Nottingham University to plan all aspects of our new venture. Whilst on one particular foray into their hallowed corridors of wisdom, I bumped into Matthew McFall who was there working on his second PhD, this one concerning the effect of wonder in learning (his first, in case you are wondering, was on the life and works of John Collier (1901–1980)). He immediately seemed to latch on to my vision for education at NUSA, especially when I started rambling on about learning spaces and creating an environment that would not only facilitate learning but also actively encourage it. Matthew's thinking – creativity combined with academic and scientific rigour – helped crystallize my own ideas around altering the way young people perceive their school and the very concept of learning. The question was, though, now I had stumbled across him so synchronistically, what was I to do with him?

Fortuntately, on the other side of the Atlantic, greedy bankers and an inadequate financial regulatory system meant that I would soon have my answer – we put him in a cupboard and called it the 'Wonder Room'.

You see, one of the effects of the global credit crunch is that we ended up with a smaller than expected budget to furnish our new academy (made all the worse by a ridiculous, expensive and less-than-transparent procurement process, but that's another story). All of which meant we had a number of small computer break-out rooms (at least, that's what the architect called them; I still think of them as cupboards with a window) but without the money to provide new computers to go in them. Knowing that nothing undermines a student's faith in a school as much as a new environment with old technology in it, I refused to countenance that alternative. Nor did I want an empty room. Both alternatives would send out the wrong message.

The answer? Abracadabra! I gave Magic Matthew the freedom to transform the space into our very own 'Wonder Room', a concept based on a fifteenth century 'cabinet of curiosity'. This has become the favourite haunt of the vast majority of our students and teachers, not to mention the many visitors we receive each month. Part of the magic that

Matthew has created in this room is to bestow it with the dimensions of Doctor Who's TARDIS. Visitors literally lose themselves in it when they enter this magical world of puzzles and illusions: a mammoth's rib, fighting cockroaches, a whale's inner ear, a Hyperscope (no, I didn't know either), an original costume from *Flash Gordon*, the world's most smelly plant, a calculating mechanical monkey, a pair of glasses that turn everything upside down, a cross-section of an oak tree showing historical dates on its numerous rings, an electronic safe that requires you to find a missing word to open it and the biggest collection of weird and wonderful puzzles I have ever seen. Each item provokes a 'Wow!', 'Why?', 'How?' or 'What on earth?' amongst wonderers of all ages. What's more, visitors regularly bring in new contributions for the room.

Of course, having an Agent of Wonder with his very own Wonder Room is just a start. We were always determined to let this positive, wonder-led attitude grow in as many ways as possible and we have developed – and continue to develop – what can only be described as a number of innovative 'wonder derivatives'. A hundred plaques with curiosity-inducing questions are hidden about the school. We have a Wonder Maze (as featured in the national press) which makes an appearance around Easter. Wonder is a key component of our schemes of work across all subjects, with much going on that I know nothing about. We even have a section of the Wonder Room where students are asked to contribute items that they claim are 'boring and mundane'. The only rule is that they must be able to, *Room 101*-style, justify why they want their object included. Interestingly, we have trouble filling this space. In other words, our children are learning that boredom is something that comes from within, and is related to your own approach and outlook, rather than from an object or subject itself. In this way we can talk openly – bravely if you like – about whether such and such a lesson is 'boring' or whether such a conclusion is more about the attitude the learner brings to it.

> Wonder is a key component of our schemes of work across all subjects.

Bravery is letting ideas grow and develop too, empowering others within the organization to take things and run with them without the fear of you looking over their shoulder. For us the theme is wonder; for you it will probably be something else. The principle is still the same though. After all, the point isn't what is in the Wonder Maze but that we have one in the first place. Whatever theme you go with, go for it with flamboyance and confidence, and make sure it sends a message across the whole school and beyond.

As an important footnote to this chapter on wonder, it is worth considering what the 'powers that be' thought of it all. After all, anyone who knows anything about the way governments run education systems will appreciate that not everyone thought a Wonder Room a good idea. Such people made it clear to me that, in order to raise exam results, all I should be doing was focusing on raising exam results. But bravery is turning your back on these powerful and influential people and doing what you know is right – raising exam results by encouraging, not enforcing, learning.

Their message was, in so many words, 'You need to get your academic achievement sorted before you start this type of thing' – something I knew deep down was quite simply back to front. I knew we had to create a climate of wonder and positivity and that then – and only then – achievement would follow. What they really needed to be saying is 'You need to start this type of thing before you get your academic achievement sorted'. Perhaps they will start to now though, especially as we have had the official seal of approval from the inspectors:

> The academy uses the expression 'the guiding principle of wonder' and genuinely promotes an enquiring mind. One of the best examples is the 'Wonder Room' (a room full of weird and wonderful artefacts from nature, science and history) which provides students with a treasure of experiences. As one student told an inspector who asked how one scientific artefact worked: 'That's the wonder of it, sir, nobody knows.'

How wonderful is that?

STEPS TO BEING BRAVE

Start a Cabinet of Curiosities in the entrance to your school. Encourage visitors to bring an item to be left in it.

17 BRAVERY IS BELIEVING THAT CREATING OPPORTUNITIES FOR SUCCESS OUTSIDE THE CLASSROOM WILL LEAD TO INCREASED SUCCESS WITHIN IT

MARATHON ACTIVITY NUMBER FIVE: CHILDREN BECOMING AUTHORS

Live long and blissful

Make the most of what you have

Nobody can go back to the beginning, anyone can make a new start

Open your heart

Put your best foot forward

Question the world but believe in yourself

Remember – you are unique

Seeing is believing

Try to accomplish little things along with big dreams

Understand the meaning of determination and desire

Voice your opinions; don't leave words unsaid

When one door closes another opens

Xylophone is a musical instrument. What's yours?

Yesterday is the past, tomorrow is the future, but today is now

Zero tolerance for the haters.
                    Saade Abdul, 'ABC … Life's the Way I Like It'

When we had the chance to link up with a successful author as part of our 'First Story' project we knew we had an opportunity to make more of it than just a well-intentioned but short-lived intervention project. The basic idea is that the children produce a number of 100-word pieces that are collated into their first collaborative book. But that would have been an easy-win 'sprint' activity which would have missed the opportunity to engage the wider community with this powerful 'marathon' opportunity. Despite the pressures to drill our children for their exams, we went to town. We held a launch party that would have rivalled any four-star London hotel (it helps that the head of our school kitchens is actually 4-star hotel standard but more of this part of our bigger plan later) with live music, exotic canapés and poetry reading. Our intention was that the children engaged with the writing project in a far more profound way than simply knocking out a piece and seeing it in print, so we involved them in every aspect of the book including designing the cover and preparing the materials to promote the launch. Our bravery paid off and it was immediately clear that the young people were engaging at a much deeper level, believing they were different and part of something very special. Which of course they were. When the book was published we also held a celebratory launch at which we showed video interpretations of some of the published work produced by another team of pupils and then we held a book signing where the audience – parents and family members – all queued to get their copy signed by the various authors. It was wonderful to watch the confidence and self-belief of the youngsters grow before our eyes.

STEPS TO BEING BRAVE

Hold a writing competition within your
school to compose a positive poem about
your school in exactly 100 words.

18 BRAVERY IS DANCING WHEN OTHERS EXPECT YOU TO LECTURE

MARATHON ACTIVITY NUMBER SIX: HANDBAGS, GLAD RAGS AND THE OCCASIONAL TEA DANCE

The pressure on me was very clear from day one. My job depended on getting the exam results up to an acceptable level (one that kept moving I might add!) in as short a time as possible. Or else. That was the chalice I accepted when I took the job. Working with the community was not, as far as 'they' were concerned, part of the day job. My heart, my gut and my research (and remember, as part of the university, all members of staff were engaged in a number of research projects) all said that trying to lift school achievement without working with the community as a whole was like bailing out a leaky boat. I knew that engaging the community was right at the heart of what we needed to do.

Simply raising achievement in individual children changes nothing in the long term for the wider community. Fact. If a school becomes fixated on having the community come through the door only for education-related projects they will miss out on a rich vein of possibilities to create new, deep and lasting relationships from which many benefits will emerge over time. It would be easy to adopt an attitude of 'We are a school, not a community centre', especially now that Ofsted no longer have to formally assess a school's community engagement. However, my view is that what we have to say is: 'We can only be a good school if we become the centre of our community'. So, what activities are you brave enough to put out there for the community in the hope that they will bring people flocking through your doors?

We found that a charity fashion show brought a completely new set of people through the academy doors, and when we ran a tea dance with a live jazz band the school hall was packed all afternoon not only with children and their parents but also their grandparents. However you get the community through the doors, make it positive and friendly and ensure that it leaves them determined to come back again!

STEPS TO BEING BRAVE

Set yourself a target to hold at least one event each term that the community wouldn't expect you to!

19 BRAVERY IS KNOWING YOU HAVE TO FEED THEIR BODIES AS WELL AS THEIR MINDS AND NOT CUT COSTS IN THE PROCESS

MARATHON ACTIVITY NUMBER SEVEN: HEALTHY BODY, HEALTHY MIND (ALSO KNOWN AS FIVE-STAR FOOD LEADS TO FIVE-STAR LEARNING!)

It's interesting (although if you ever see me, maybe not surprising) that some of our most successful 'marathon' activities have been linked to food. An army may march on its stomach but I think a school learns on its stomach. One of the first appointments I was fortunate enough to make was that of a quite amazing chef (and yes, he is a chef, not a cook), who transformed our lunchtime menu.

It is worth noting, at this juncture, that you don't get extraordinary people through an ordinary interview processes. We didn't advertise for a 'school cook' but for a 'head chef'. Then, once we had short-listed, we ensured there would be no boring interview panels. Instead there was a live spreadsheet exercise to check they could balance the books and then a timed *Ready, Steady, Cook* style 'cook off' in which each candidate had to prepare an attractive healthy meal for a set number for a budget of £5 plus a 'design a series of snack-type meals from this basket of ingredients' exercise. Are you brave enough to completely redesign your interview process to identify and attract extraordinary people?

The result of this process is that we have a world-class member of the team who believes wholeheartedly in what we are trying to achieve (remember the concept of self-similarity I mentioned in Chapter 12?) and who supports our work through his own particular domain (and don't ever mention Turkey Twizzlers to him or he'll come at you with a spatula).

In the same way that families who eat together share many benefits, I feel the same is true of schools. Staff are allowed to eat for free if they sit with the pupils and the wonderful quality of the food has ensured that we have over 80% take-up of this offer. The whole eating experience is an incredibly positive one and NUSA has become a very popular destination for lunchtime meetings with various elements of the school community. If you are ever looking for a community police officer at lunchtime you know where to come.

> Let your staff eat for free if they sit with the pupils.

STEPS TO BEING BRAVE

Ask your chef (no 'cooks' please!) to hold a Gourmet Tuesday with a menu containing unfamiliar dishes.

20 BRAVERY IS NEVER USING THOSE COMMERCIALLY PRODUCED 'SUCCESS' POSTERS, TRUSTING YOUR STUDENTS TO COME UP WITH SOMETHING TEN TIMES BETTER AND TURNING THAT INTO ARTWORK AROUND THE SCHOOL WHEN THEY DO

MARATHON ACTIVITY NUMBER EIGHT: CELEBRATING PUPIL WORK

Throughout the academy, the words of staff and pupils are used in preference to commercially produced words of inspiration. The poem below, which describes the journey of our school through the eyes of one of our Year 11 children, has been printed out on a 6 m x 3 m banner and displayed in 'The Street' – an open, covered communal area at the heart of the school. It serves as a source of inspiration on a daily basis for all of us, children and adults alike.

> Looking past the raindrops I could see the jigsaw of mismatched concrete and the confetti of peeling paintwork,
>
> Kids with no respect were climbing up the barred windows in the downpour of rain.
>
> But glancing towards the creaking scaffolding not too far away was the start of new hope.

A building confidence we could be someone.

But there were always a few who were resistant;

Wanting something for themselves but not wanting to change.

People around us were not able to see the same kids achieving in the world.

Others were looking down on the pupils even though they were the ones who would change the future.

But that was a while ago,

And now we realize how lucky we are.

With Courage, Courtesy and Aspiration we created NUSA.

Lauren Cater (age 15)

None of the marathon activities you have read about above are unique to our school. Although I am incredibly proud of everything we have achieved at NUSA, I share them with you not out of pride but in order to reassure; not to show you we are special but to reinforce the view that, at a time when there is more pressure than ever on school leaders to focus on better results, and nothing but results, we should never compromise on what we believe in or lack the courage to invest in the bigger, wider picture. In doing so, the results will come. Or, to go back to our Ofsted report one final time:

> Since the opening of the academy leaders have been determined to be reflective and researched-based, appreciating the need to make rapid improvement whilst not losing sight of building for long-term success.

So come on – be brave, don't simply focus on the targets you are given – take a chance to do those wonderful, exciting, slightly barmy things which remind you why you love this job so much!

STEPS TO BEING BRAVE

Decide on at least one 'off the wall', barmy, left-field thing to do before the end of this term.

BRAVE
LEADERSHIP

21 BRAVERY IS KNOWING THAT SCHOOL LEADERSHIP IS NOT ALL ABOUT YOU

Please God, let me be doing the right thing today.

The head teacher's daily prayer

Maybe the question isn't 'What type of head are you?' but 'What type of head are you being today and is it the type best suited to the current demands of the job?' You may have been up all night practising your best nurturing approach for the following day but, as any humble head will know, there is more affecting the mood of a school each day than the head's will.

In fact, based on the research I am undertaking as part of my PhD, with our co-sponsor Nottingham University, I have identified six different factors acting on a school at any given time:

As you can see, your own personality is not the only factor. Your leadership output depends on the answers to all, some of or much more than the following questions:

- Where are you on the process of change you are going through?

- What are the current strengths and weaknesses of your staff?

- What are their current expectations?

- What are the perceptions of the school by the community?

- What are the perceptions of the school by the staff?

- What are the perceptions of the school by the pupils?

- Do the pupils want to come to school?

- Do they feel safe?

- Do they enjoy their learning?

- Does the building appear loved?

- Does the building restrict learning?

- Do the governors have an accurate view of the school?

- Do the governors know what they want the school to achieve?

- Do the governors understand what modern schooling is for?

- Do the staff enjoy coming to work?

- What is the turnover rate of staff at the school?

- What is the attendance rate of staff at the school?

- How many of the staff can deliver outstanding lessons with regularity?

- How many of the staff are happy being satisfactory?

- Do you bounce out of bed each morning?

- Do you have a passion for change?

- Where is your school on its journey to the 'top of the mountain'?

- Where are you on your own personal journey?

In my thirty-plus years in education I have seen many great leaders and, on occasions, a few outstanding ones. However, even some of the best ran into trouble when they underestimated the interplay of all these factors in a school's success and equated their own leadership with a school's achievement. These heads soon have difficulties when they try to replicate their successful style in a new school, one in which the other relevant factors are very different.

Being brave is important. However, we should always take care to bear in mind that it is only one small step along the continuum from stupid. You have been warned!

STEPS TO BEING BRAVE

Identify the bravest thing you have done this month. And then the stupidest. Work out why the brave one wasn't stupid and the stupid one wasn't brave!

22 BRAVERY IS KNOWING WHAT SORT OF LEADER YOU ARE

Who is the best head for the job? Or, to be braver about it, are you really the best head for your particular school?

People will always claim they want the best head for their school (advertisements frequently want new leaders to be 'outstanding', 'inspirational', 'world-class' or 'exceptional', and who can blame them). However, whilst in tennis you get a ranking of the top ten players in the world at any given time, such an exercise would be pointless in the education system, even if it were possible (although it would feature more British names I'm sure!). Successful school leadership covers a wide range of styles and I have seen a number of heads who have been very successful in one school but who have had much more difficulty in different surroundings. This suggests that successful leadership is not a fixed affair but instead is inextricably linked to the school setting itself. What works in one school would simply be the entirely wrong strategy in another. What's more, as schools grow and change, an approach that is successful when leading a school through one stage of its life may end up being the very thing that holds it back later in the life cycle. Most successful leaders are, therefore, successful because they can adopt a range of styles to best fit the time and place in which they are working. What's more, they know (or at least are prepared to listen to people who do know) when the time is right to change the way they do things and move to a different model of leadership.

> Most successful leaders are successful because they can adopt a range of styles to best fit the time and place in which they are working.

Whilst there are many clever people writing some great (and some not so great) books on leadership in education, I have put together a list of the four different sorts of leadership style I have witnessed on my travels: the Fat Controller, the Nurturer, the Corporate Executive and the Gardener. See where you fit in and remember: it is not a case of which type of leadership (or combination of types) is best but which is best suited to the school and community it serves at any given time. And, of course, whether you have the bravery to do anything about it …

STEPS TO BEING BRAVE

Write down which movie character would best match your leadership style and why.

23 BRAVERY CAN BE BREAKING THE RULES, BUT SOMETIMES IT IS STICKING TO THEM

THE FAT CONTROLLER

This is a head who stands by the conviction that there are a clear set of rules that can bring about transformation, rules that are tried and tested and have been shown to work in other surroundings. It is the 'This is what needs to be fixed and this is what will fix it' approach and is often the strategy used in a school turnaround situation where the new head – often referred to in the press as a 'super-head' – has been brought in to transform a struggling school and make that difference quickly. Because of this leader-centric approach, all change is instigated, driven and evaluated by the head who quickly becomes the centre for everything.

> A Fat Controller has the 'This is what needs to be fixed and this is what will fix it' approach.

Here are the five steps often followed by the Fat Controller.

STEP 1: DEVELOP ORDER

Quickly make your presence felt. Change should be immediate and obvious. Alter the times of the school day, periods in the week, lunchtime arrangements or term arrangements – anything that sends a quick and clear message that there's a new head in town and things aren't what they used to be. The Fat Controller must be seen as the driver of change and should engineer some clear victories in the first few weeks. Some difficult pupils should be made examples of and new regimes implemented. The head's office should be placed in the most prominent position available and then he or she should meet as many parents as possible in order to spread the message of change. The public face of the school should be carefully managed, with a regimented protocol on all external communications. All letters leaving the premises should be read and approved by the head to ensure that no remnants of 'old ways' are allowed to remain. (It is surprisingly easy for letters to be sent out whose general wording has not changed in decades. I imagine many reading this will have been in leadership meetings when an imminent parents' evening is remembered, someone is assigned the task of arranging it and their first task is simply to change the dates on last year's letter!)

STEP 2: OUTLINE THE RULES TO BE FOLLOWED

A new behaviour code should be created and clearly displayed on each classroom wall and in pupil planners. It is important to make sure that all pupils understand the rule of cause and effect. In other words, if you fail to follow rules there will be repercussions; if you follow the rules there will be prizes. It will also be desirable to make a few simple rules for staff which should be as unambiguous as possible. A series of assemblies outlining the new way things are done around here should be held to ensure that all pupils and staff receive the same message.

However, a room full of staff receiving the same message will each internalize and then implement it in varied ways, some more consistently than others. And where you have a rule that some teachers follow and others don't, you don't have a rule. Therefore it is essential for the expected actions to be modelled so everyone is clear what the rule is. And once you have successfully modelled it, model it again. Some say a behaviour is not learnt until it has been repeated at least sixteen times.

At NUSA we identified a problem with pupils' use of mobile phones and the way they were a distraction in lessons. By implementing a strict rule, which we then all adhered to faithfully, the problem was solved within a week. Any pupil seen using a phone in lessons had it removed from them and only their parents/guardians could retrieve it. This retrieval could not take place less than twenty-four hours after the transgression, something akin to asking a young person not to breathe for a day! Once pupils found that this was not an empty threat, but a new way of acting for all staff, the problem all but disappeared. And quickly!

STEP 3: DEVELOP HIERARCHICAL LEADERSHIP

Accountability and responsibility are the watchwords for this style of school change. It is vital that all levels of leadership within the organization have an identical perception of the steps needed for change. The leader must have ways of ensuring the message is clear and unambiguous. All teams should have representation that comes back to the centre; so, for example, minutes of departmental meetings should be read by the head and acted upon quickly. Information should be disseminated and gathered through a pyramid structure with expected behaviours made explicit at every level.

One school I worked in went as far as drawing a map of every duty patrol and then checking the staff rigidly abided by this structure. Staff had little power of discretion but the school was safe and pupils and staff expressed a much-needed sense of relief at the new clarity regarding what was expected of them. To achieve this, it is vital that the head's vision is expressed very clearly and that there is no opportunity for misunderstanding regarding the direction of travel. The key must be a relentless focus on teaching and learning matched with a never-ending feedback loop of observation, evaluation, innovation and staff development. Nothing less than high quality is acceptable for every lesson and the responsibility for this is integrated into every level of the management structure.

STEP 4: PRACTISE DRILLS, REWARD COMPLIANCE AND PUNISH DISOBEDIENCE

This type of leadership is one whose message must be reinforced – and enforced – repeatedly. Success is founded upon rapidly providing a credible and strong framework around which school life can be built. There should be a clear and consistent structure from the start of the day to the end. Pupils should be met on arrival and anyone not appearing ready for work should be dealt with quickly. Many pupils will find the rigid structure stress reducing and will be more than happy to comply with its demands. Rewards for achievement should be large, emphasized and preferably public. Failure by individuals to adopt, and adapt to, new practices should result in swift and strong repercussions – but beware. Turning miscreants into heroes is a risk and will be counter-productive.

Some staff will find the demands of such a tight regime stressful, as the teaching profession has long been one that prizes individuality. However, this type of change must be focused on the pupil (especially the pupils' achievements as recorded in the data that is published publically) rather than the staff. If the staff's resistance is an obstruction to improving things for the learners then it is down to the brave head to do something about it. As the Head of Ofsted Michael Wilshaw is quoted as saying, and in a tone that is not without its controversy: 'if anyone says to you that "staff morale is at an all-time low" you will know you are doing something right' (Stewart, 2011).

Not that I am advocating the sort of leadership that goes out of its way to make working life unnecessarily hard for staff; quite the opposite. But what I am saying is that the brave head will need to do whatever it is that needs to be done to guarantee the optimum learning environment that will ensure all pupils get the best possible grades.

STEP 5: MAINTAIN SUCCESS

Once you have created the type of dramatic change that can be 'forced' upon a school in this regimented way, there is then one important thing left to do. You must keep the momentum going … and going … and going …

STEPS TO BEING BRAVE

Identify times that you have adopted the behaviour of the Fat Controller and what happened as a result.

24 BRAVERY IS FOCUSING ON YOUR COMMUNITY'S SUCCESS AND NOT YOUR OWN

THE NURTURER

This type of head has amazing integrity. They have no need at all for the external pressure of government targets or inspections; they require no motivation other than the young lives in their care and the opportunity to give each child the best possible chance. The ethos of the school is a relentless focus on each individual in a way that includes – but goes beyond – exam results. It is an approach that can be summed up in the following steps.

STEP 1: IDENTIFY THE INDIVIDUAL

When beginning in a new school or new role the Nurturer will divert attention away from him or herself and onto the young people served by the school. The staff meetings will not be focused on rules and regulations but on the pupils: Who are they? What are their hopes and dreams? How can the staff tap into these and help children be all they can be? The true Nurturer will not want the staff to accept lower standards for the more needy pupils. They will be keen to make sure that the targets are aspirational and that no one is coasting. Equally, they will be almost fanatical in their desire to ensure that teachers are 'scaffolding' the learning and that no pupils are left to fend for themselves.

STEP 2: IDENTIFY THE GOAL

If the first step is to understand the skills and current achievements of each pupil, the next stage is to decide on an appropriate goal for each individual in the school. In this way, nurturing heads may sometimes appear confrontational towards the government (and even the governors) as they will refuse to accept an externally enforced goal simply because that is what someone tells them to do. For them, the only suitable goal will be one that makes sense not only for every child but also within the context of the individual story of each unique community. After all, polices tend to be very broad brush strokes – blunt tools to forge out of schools whatever it is that happens to be in the mind of the Secretary of State for Education at any given time.

The nurturing head will make sure they know the back story to their school's past achievements and future ambitions and use them to work together to create a common, specific vision for the school and all its stakeholders. They set a path from which the school will not deviate, regardless of the latest trends in qualifications, PISA results or league tables. Their response to the latest shift in the ranking of vocational qualifications or introduction of the English Baccalaureate will be to ask questions such as, 'If the courses we were doing last week were carefully chosen and right for our learners, then why do these latest pronouncement render them useless?' Having carefully thought through a course of action, the brave Nurturer will not be diverted from doing what they feel is right for the children – and adults – in their care and for the wider community as a whole.

STEP 3: TRAVEL TOGETHER TOWARDS THE GOAL

The next phase of development for the Nurturer's school is to foster a strong and inclusive team spirit. Work will be focused on celebrating the success of others – identifying their strengths rather than finding weaknesses. Staff and pupils will engage in communal activities, residential trips and projects that encourage empathy, understanding and growth. For example:

■ The school develops links with one or more areas of the world that it feels it can help. Children work together to raise money through a variety of activities for the link community and you may even organize visits of young people and teachers. Many of these projects are of a cross-curricular nature and may involve non-curriculum skills and possibilities. The role of each individual in being part of a 'greater good' is emphasized and a practical self-belief is celebrated.

■ A whole-school project based around activities such as 'Random Acts of Kindness' (see www.randomactsofkindness.org for more details). For example, pupils and staff are expected to participate by carrying out 'selfless acts' (if there is such a thing) in one, more or all of four main categories:

- For family and friends, e.g.

  ▲ Leave a note for a parent or other key family member telling them how appreciated they are

  ▲ Spend time with a younger sibling or aging relation

  ▲ Make or buy a special treat for a close friend

- For strangers, e.g.

  ▲ Make Christmas cards for the members of a residential home

  ▲ Leave a reading book for others to pick up in a cafe

  ▲ Help people with mobility difficulties carry shopping to the bus or car

- For the environment, e.g.

  ▲ Plant trees in local disused areas

  ▲ Start a scheme at a local supermarket helping to reuse carrier bags

  ▲ Help locals save money and packaging by buying in bulk

● For yourself, e.g.

▲ Learn a language or a new skill

▲ Learn how to bake cakes (and then share them with the elderly for a double whammy!)

▲ Volunteer to spend time at a local residential home or old-age pensioner group or charity

These are just a few suggestions and could be substituted with hundreds of other innovative ideas emanating from schools across the country. What's more, if the Nurturer is a new head, it is important that they build on the embers of already existing projects, especially as these will most likely have strong personal relationships already underpinning them.

In a successful school that is not under the watchful eye of people like Her Majesty's Inspectors, such activities are always seen as welcome contributions to the life of the establishment. It would appear odd for similar endeavours not to be taking place in one form or another. The logic seems to be, 'Charity begins at home, so sort out your grades and then start to think about helping others'. The brave head, though, knows this isn't necessarily the case. Even though some may judge this type of focus to be an unnecessary distraction from the 'core purpose' of teaching and learning, and say so vocally and publically, a brave Nurturer knows differently and has the courage to act on that belief. Rather than waiting for indicators like grades to improve before they embark on such projects, they know that it is activities like these that will actually serve to improve grades (along with much else besides). One way they do this is to give core learning a context. If pupils are excited and emotionally engaged in activities that are not simply focused on them, then they are developing an important belief in their ability to change not only their destiny but that of others. This translates into a very powerful motivation to learn.

We sometimes become blinkered by the content-heavy nature of our curriculum and its associated assessment system. Learning is simply what can be measured in a clear and factual way, and what can be measured most easily are grades. These 'facts' then become our key motivation. Working in this way means that children can lose sight of – or never glimpse at all – the real purpose of becoming educated citizens. 'Because it's in the test' is a very poor justification to be spending your life doing something; all the more so when you are from a background where tests are regarded as, at best, pointless and, at worse, a constant public provider of the evidence of your own and your community's failures. But when the learning that is taking place is tied into a real-life application, one in which pupils have a vested emotion, then their motivation and progress improves dramatically.

STEP 4: CELEBRATE THE JOURNEY

The Nurturer is not focused on gaining recognition for themselves, nor on making a model of transformational schooling which can be replicated across the country. (This is more the domain of the Fat Controller for whom each school in which they weave their 'magic' is a stepping-stone to the next and, beyond that, who knows?) The goal of the Nurturer is quite simply and unselfishly to help the community in which they work. And in so many schools, the starting point is to focus on the community's own sense of self-belief. As Samuel Johnson once said, 'Self-confidence is the first requisite to great undertakings' and the Nurturer will actively seek to set up a feedback mechanism in which successes are amplified and celebrated amongst the community, thus encouraging further self-belief, in turn leading to further progress.

> The goal of the Nurturer is quite simply and unselfishly to help the community in which they work.

STEPS TO BEING BRAVE

Identify times that you have adopted the behaviour of the Nurturer and what happened as a result.

25 BRAVERY IS RECOGNIZING YOUR FAULTS

THE CORPORATE EXECUTIVE

Sharp pin-stripe suit, designer leather shoes and a slim, elegant briefcase are all signs that you are in the presence of the Corporate Executive style of head teacher. The aura surrounding these leaders is one of unshakeable self-belief and a daunting self-confidence. There is no room for doubting the approach of such a head. Their confidence in where they are going is matched only by their belief in how to get there. Time is of the essence and there is little room for uncertainty as there is space for individuality. After all, why think for yourself when the answers are all there in the bookcase or, as is becoming increasingly the case, in the academy chain handbook?

> It's about the confidence in knowing where you're going matched with the confidence in how to get there.

These days the Corporate Executive is often found in the academy chain and he or she has a clear road map to follow when it comes to the transformation of a school, which is based on the path followed by the organization's sister institutions. There is not a great deal of importance awarded to an individual's context or community. It's all about moving away as quickly as possible from the 'failure' that went before. And the best way, indeed the only way, to achieve this is to implement solutions that have worked elsewhere in what are deemed to be comparable schools. This approach, sometimes referred to as 'the McDonald's Way', follows three steps.

STEP 1: SITE SELECTION AND PREPARATION

This is an important step in the Corporate Executive's plans. The less complex the location, the more suitable the timing; the more appropriate the arena for change, the quicker and more dramatic that change will appear. The reputation of the whole organization is a key factor in its success, so quick wins will be essential – and the more dramatic the better. The new site must rapidly signal affinity to the central body. This is a time for corporate badging, a new uniform, new name, new colours and new history. The success of affiliated organizations is celebrated and posters and banners remind staff and pupils of their new opportunity. Policies and procedures are introduced with speed and the leadership structure is developed in line with the ethos of the chain.

STEP 2: REPLICATE THE MODEL

It is important to give the school direction and purpose quickly. School councils will be set up and school captains and presidents appointed. Pupils will be encouraged to signify their new allegiances by developing posters, signs and mottos. Whilst the main structure in the academy chain will require similarity across the schools, there will always be areas of development that can be handed over to the pupil voice. The engagement of pupils has been identified as a key step in any major transformation.

Staff commitment is obviously a vital factor in success and the Corporate Executive will wish to maximize this. By commitment, however, what is meant is the preparedness to do things 'the way we do things in this organization' and the head will often be impatient for staff to get the message. There will be a staff code of practice and any individuals who feel uncomfortable with any aspect of it will be encouraged to leave. A clear and regulated observation regime will be implemented from an early stage, something that will inevitably lead to the quick 'movement' of some individuals. Any leaders with a strong involvement prior to the 'new way' will be expected to publically distance themselves from the institution's past. At Nottingham University Samworth Academy, language connected to a positive future was the only language that was acceptable, and I have to admit to finishing many assemblies with a spoof of the mobile phone advert: 'The future's bright, the future's NUSA!'

> The engagement of pupils has been identified as a key step in any major transformation.

STEP 3: ADAPTION AND FINE TUNING

The Corporate Executive is an interesting role, and not one that will appeal to everyone. On one hand, it is a high profile, high power position (if that is your thing) and everything within an institution will revolve around you. On the other hand, the path for improvement that the institution will take is pretty well predetermined by what has worked elsewhere in the past. Similarly, because success is assured by the use of a proven system, if your school doesn't hit the targets in the allotted time it is clearly your fault, not the system's.

Linked to that is the fact that, although all heads should need an Equity card to do their job properly, often needing to turn out convincing performances in a whole variety of roles, the Corporate Executive has a very tight script and must deliver their lines in the expected way. There is little room, if any, for improvisation. Part of the process also involves regular benchmarking between the new organization and existing ones within the academy group. Inevitably this may present the new school with a challenge as not all schools develop in a linear way, despite the best intentions (and claims) of politicians.

The need to always show improvement and not let the side down will usually cause the Corporate Executive to make interpretation B. There is no place for 'blips' in their cut-throat world.

STEPS TO BEING BRAVE

Identify times that you have adopted the behaviour of the Corporate Executive and what happened as a result.

26 BRAVERY IS CREATING THE SPACE FOR YOUR PLANTS TO GROW

THE GARDENER

This leader is an idealist who believes that a beautiful garden can be created in the most unlikely of places. It is the approach that I felt was most needed when it came to my work at NUSA so I share it with you in that context. The work of the Gardener occurs in six steps.

> A beautiful garden can be created in the most unlikely of places.

STEP 1: CLEAR THE GROUND

The Gardener will evaluate the successes of the school and protect them, where possible making a virtue of them. They will indentify the things that are blocking growth (or even worse, damaging the achievement) and remove them. A brave head is always prepared to be brutal when it comes to getting rid of what clearly doesn't work, no matter how many years it has been going on. After all, a large number of the school's activities may in fact be 'noise', contributing nothing to its overall success.

In my early days at NUSA some 'officials' made it clear that they believed a number of the staff I was inheriting were, as it were, 'weeds that should be removed'. Thank heavens I was allowed to use my gardening skills to recognize that what I actually had was what I can only describe as a number of feature plants that just hadn't been given the environment in which to flourish.

STEP 2: CREATE THE CONDITIONS FOR GROWTH

One of my two sponsors is Sir David Samworth (of Ginsters' fame) and one of the strategies that has helped him to make his family business into one of the most successful in the country is what he calls 'the Samworth Way'. This is known by all his employees as the 'PQP' philosophy – People, Quality, Profit. In that order. It became clear right from the early days of NUSA that we would benefit from a similar strategy in order to work with and support our staff and students in developing a consistent culture of high expectations and equally high standards.

We set about working with the staff to create a positive culture focused on the success of the pupils. We regularly reminded them of the reasons they went into the job in the first place and we developed a real sense of doing things our way, 'the NUSA Way'. This was a simple set of guidelines for how pupils would behave with each other and with staff and also, importantly, how staff would behave towards students and each other. Rather than wrap up these expectations in some arcane behaviour policy, we summed them up in a way that would be as easy to remember as to execute:

Courtesy, Courage and Aspiration.

All staff and pupils were then expected to build these three attributes into their daily work, behaviours and attitudes. And this meant all staff, including administrative personnel, kitchen staff, the caretaker and, of course, the leadership team.

STEP 3: SOW THE SEEDS

The Gardener will want to introduce some key new projects that are likely to produce some quick wins. If the school doesn't have a uniform consider bringing one in – not because uniforms produce results on their own (despite what certain newspapers assert) but because they can be a very powerful symbol of change. Alternatively, start new rewards schemes. (If you haven't encountered Vivo I would recommend investigating it at www.vivomiles.com. It is a powerful online system that is an innovative fusion of a good school merit system with air miles, in which good behaviour is rewarded with 'virtual' points which are collected to allow children to enjoy actual rewards ranging from stationery to iPods.) As you introduce the new ideas, remember to be on the lookout when it comes to cultivating existing ones too, as we did with the record label at NUSA (see Chapter 14).

STEP 4: DO THE LITTLE THINGS DAILY – WATER, FERTILIZE AND ENCOURAGE GROWTH

The Gardener will focus on the small things that enable staff and pupils to believe that growth and change are possible. Offer small bursaries (between £100 and £250) to any staff who can develop an innovative community project. (e.g. a literacy garden for local families or a collection of memories from elderly groups in the community). Celebrate even small achievements by pupils, creating an atmosphere where praise is a perfectly normal part of the day-to-day life of the school. At NUSA we held a staff innovation competition where staff members were asked to nominate ideas from their own new practice and then, after they had all been observed, the 'winning ideas' (judged by the leadership team and measured by outcomes) were given shopping vouchers. One winner introduced a series of calendars celebrating pupil work and another introduced plenaries based on Maslow's hierarchy in all her lessons.

> Celebrate even small achievements by pupils, creating an atmosphere where praise is a perfectly normal part of the day-to-day life of the school.

Ensure a regular newsletter is produced and sent home and make sure you use this as a device for sharing a range of successes with parents and the wider community. Enter pupils and staff into as many competitions as possible. For example, every local newspaper, council and national body seems to have a 'Young Person of the Year' award. Just being entered for these and sharing this success around the school brings a huge boost to self-belief and self-respect. Ensure any positive comments from the community echo around the school and that pupils identified in a positive way are celebrated and praised in as many ways as possible.

STEP 5: REMOVE THE WEEDS AND SUPPORT AREAS OF POOR GROWTH

Having given all the staff and pupils the chance to grow and develop now is the time for the Gardener to take stock of the whole school development. Identify individuals and groups that haven't taken the opportunity to grow and may be responsible for holding others back. They are probably the ones who have not accepted the 'new way', who have not made the appropriate adjustments and improvements in teaching and learning, and have remained focused on the negatives rather than the positives. They are almost invariably 'half-empty' people. It is important for you (and them) that they are helped to realize that the new way is the only way that is acceptable. Some may have the will but have not yet acquired the skills required to bring about changes in classroom practice.

Coaching is a very effective way of helping these staff move to the next level of performance. Ensure that all teachers are aware of what an outstanding lesson looks like, so there are no excuses, and then hold to them account. This is different from everyone teaching to the 'academy book', although, at times, some simple 'Do it this way' instruction may provide a helpful start.

However, where the individual has no recognition of the need for change and no desire for improvement, then I'm afraid the brave head whose focus is the success of the school and the community as a whole has no choice but to reach for the trusty garden tools and begin the process of weeding …

STEP 6: ENJOY THE GARDEN – TENDING AS NEEDED

Perfection is not a destination so don't wait until you get there to feel good about what you are achieving. There may be certain goals you are working towards (the first set of public exam results and the next major Ofsted inspection are two that spring to mind) but don't wait for them in order to recognize and celebrate all you have achieved and the how far along the journey you have all come. Ensuring that the school's success is not measured simply in exam results is a key part of this approach. For example, when you start to see changes in self-belief then they are worth celebrating. At NUSA I have seen clear evidence of pupils responding positively to the success of others and to stories of achievement in the academy. Write newspaper articles, offer showcases for national conferences and encourage visits from far and wide. Never hide your light under a bushel!

STEPS TO BEING BRAVE

Identify times that you have adopted the behaviour of the Gardener and what happened as a result.

27 BRAVERY IS KNOWING YOURSELF – AND BEING HONEST ENOUGH TO ACT ACCORDINGLY

SO WHAT TYPE OF HEAD ARE YOU?

If you were to put the four styles of leadership into a graph it would look something like this:

Individual pupil success

NURTURER	FAT CONTROLLER
GARDENER	CORPORATE EXECUTIVE

Free style — Directed

School success

Use this graph to plot where you are at any given time and to act as a check and balance to help you decide if you are in the right quadrant for what is being asked of you. The brave head knows that he or she will have to jump into a quadrant they are not comfortable with if the need arises – a need driven by ensuring that the best decisions are taken in the interests of the learners and their community.

Of course, the answer, if we are honest, is none of them all of the time and all of them some of the time. The implication for us mere mortals is that if we don't fit into a specific profile we won't succeed as a leader.

We measure ourselves against distilled ideals of perfect leadership and then we see our own weaknesses, the mistakes we make every day, the battles we lose and the insecurities we experience. We start to believe that we simply aren't in the same league as the leader role-models we so admire . Well, stop it! I mean it, *stop*! The reality is that the great leaders we so revere felt – or still feel – just as fallible and full of self-doubt as you do. In fact, I am convinced that one of the most reliable characteristics of a great leader is doubt in their own ability. It ensures a necessary grounding in everything they do.

So, why do we all allow ourselves to be so easily manipulated? Firstly, success is rarely as straightforward as it is portrayed. 'Experts' visit successful schools looking for simplistic answers and, sure enough, that is what they find: simple answers. If the leader has an extreme habit or behaviour then this becomes a key part of the success criteria, as opposed to what is more likely, an incidental action. I have over 300 silly and outrageous ties that I never reuse in the same term. I think we would all agree that these play no part in any success I have had, but they are part of the leader I choose to be. If you hate ties that doesn't make you less of a leader, does it?

> Do what you think is right, in the way you think it should be done and have the bravery to follow through on your beliefs.

Secondly, I am greatly concerned by the implication that there is a single mould for successful leadership. I have seen some wonderful educational leaders, but do you know what the single biggest thing I learn from them is? That there is no single biggest thing I can learn from them. There is no magical leadership DNA, no formula, no one set of skills I can learn or mimic. What there is though is a group of interesting individuals who have made the most of time and place in their own way. What they all show is the ability to do what they think is the right thing to do in the way in which they think it should be done, and have the bravery to follow through on their beliefs. That's it! Really, that's all there is to it – and don't let them tell you any different. In fact, if I were asked to write my four lessons for brave school leadership they would be as follows:

Rule 1: Be yourself.

Rule 2: Be yourself.

Rule 3: Be yourself.

Rule 4: There are no rules.

> Be yourself.

The four types of school leader I have described are simply an extended spectrum. There are, after all, probably as many types of successful leader as there are successful leaders, and as many successful leaders as there are successful schools. That said, 'know thyself' has been part of human wisdom for several thousand years, and it can have its uses in identifying what sort of leader you are being at any given time. For myself, I know that, on the whole, I like to think of myself a Gardener with nurturing tendencies (except for the odd time when I choose to be a Fat Controller). How about that for leadership style!

STEPS TO BEING BRAVE

Give yourself a grade out of ten for each of the four styles of leadership that you have used in the last term. Decide if and how this balance should change over the next term.

28 BRAVERY IS SERVING THE COMMUNITY AROUND YOU

Isn't what we all want to serve the community? Yet you wouldn't think this was the case if you looked at the approaches of some of the new 'chain' schools. They seem to have only the desire for success based upon the philosophy of replication without adaption. They seem to believe they have the DNA for success – the magic bullet – that can then be copied anywhere. To some of us this seems a tad egotistical. To know 'what is best' for another community, and then to impose it, has echoes of some of Britain's worst behaviour from our murky colonial past.

Surely, what we want is to help the community find its own success. I challenge anyone to show me a community that doesn't have something to be proud of. Once you find this, you then celebrate it and do so in as public a way as possible. Then pupils and parents start to believe in their own potential and an unshakeable belief in the transformational powers of the organization quickly grows.

One side effect is that it will rapidly increase the number of applications to your school as word of your 'desirability' gets out. This is a different story from the situation faced by the school change brigade who go in for the quick win by attracting a certain type of parent, one with a tradition of valuing academic achievement. Like turning the local pub into an upmarket sushi bar, do you achieve results by changing the clientele or by working with the community that the establishment was set up to serve and helping to change for the better the way they think and act? Your conscience will decide …

BRAVE
RESEARCH

29 BRAVERY IS NOT BEING SCARED TO LOOK THE RESEARCH IN THE EYE

Working in a university-sponsored academy has given me a real insight into a world I knew little about. I know the 'remote spires on the hill' is a tired metaphor, but if I am honest, the concern that a university would have nothing to offer to support the day-to-day running of a real school was still on my mind, at least subconsciously. I was delighted to discover that in fact universities (or at least Nottingham University) have become vibrant and innovative hubs that want to make their thinking and findings real and accessible for the local community. I am not saying that stereotypical academics do not exist, they do. I have witnessed them in action – people for whom the information is the end rather than the beginning of their work. However, they are vastly in a minority. Most people I have met through the university are amongst the most excited, interesting and interested I have ever come across. I encourage you to forge links with whichever academic institution is closest to you. Hopefully you will find, as I did, a body of motivated people whose specialisms – whether education or archaeology – only truly come alive when they have an application in the real world. In my experience, this has been hugely positive and has helped to produce a school-wide understanding that research is not simply a static entity to be consumed but an essential part of a school that wants to be all that it can be.

The leadership team at Nottingham University Samworth Academy has gained a communal understanding of the benefits of becoming a research-focused organization through every one of them having the chance to take a Masters in Teaching and Learning. Through working together on a wide range of research material, the group has come to understand the strengths and weaknesses, the power and the pitfalls of proper academic research. The process has been demystified and everyone has begun to carry out his or her own practitioner research. We have learnt to avoid one of two knee-jerk responses to research so common in schools – either swallow it all, lock, stock and barrel as the 'magic bullet' they so wish it was, or ignore it completely. There is rarely a simple solution to a complex educational problem and quality research often provides more questions than answers. But doing nothing when there is evidence that things can be better is not the answer either.

I have embarked on a PhD looking at the process of change at NUSA as the developments occur, rather than from the more traditional sanctuary of a successful point in time in the future and looking back. I am trying to capture a full range of data that can be used to investigate the changes we have made and are making. This process is made more complicated by my own position within the organization. To be honest, it is difficult to maintain a truly independent viewpoint from where I'm sitting on a day-to-day basis. However, with careful planning and thought, unique insight can be gained from analysing the changes taking place at the school as they happen, and I am hopeful that over the next five years my understanding will become much richer still.

For those of you who haven't embarked on a doctorate (yet!), one of the first things you do before you set to work on your research proper is to prepare a 'confirmation of status' paper. This detailed document – it took me about a year to prepare – outlines my intended work but also summarizes much of the current literature connected to the area under investigation. In this section of the book, therefore, I will share some of that research with you to show you the academic underpinnings of brave headship as well as saving you many hundreds of hours of reading into the bargain. What follows is some of the most up-to-date thinking on educational leadership from some of the world's leading thinkers, all designed to help you in your own journey to brave – but not gung-ho – school leadership.

STEPS TO BEING BRAVE

Circulate a short piece of academic writing to all your staff and set aside time in a meeting to discuss its implications for your school.

30 BRAVERY IS A NUMBER OF FACTORS

What comes through in the research is that you can effectively boil down successful brave leadership into four factors over which you wield considerable influence, and all of which have a part to play when it comes to your success.

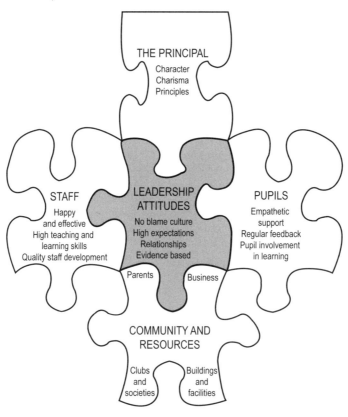

I will take you through each part of the brave leadership jigsaw and what is highlighted in the latest research. I will adopt my best academic tone as we are in the presence of greatness here, people like Christopher Day, Kenneth Leithwood, David Hargreaves, Dean Fink, Michael Fullan, Tim Brighouse and at least two researchers named Harris, neither of whom are any relation. I even throw in some Sir Michael Wilshaw for good measure. Hopefully, like me, you will begin to see the patterns in the jigsaw emerge and start to grasp just how effective a strong, thoughtful, confident but open-minded school leader can be. And then, who knows, maybe next time you will be the object of the research.

STEPS TO BEING BRAVE

Start a research board in the staffroom. Encourage staff to put interesting articles on it.

31 BRAVERY IS KNOWING WHETHER YOU'RE LEADING FROM THE FRONT OR THE CENTRE OF THE SCHOOL

The lack of scientific evidence for the importance of the role of the head teacher seems to have been compensated for by the sheer volume of literature available on this topic.

In his 1994 book Moon challenges:

> Indeed I am still looking for a research study which demonstrates convincingly that the head teacher was not at the centre of things and yet the school, for which they were responsible, still functioned effectively. (Moon and Shelton-Mayes, 1994: 321)

In my view it is important to distinguish between being at the centre of the organization and being at the front. When we talk about 'leading from the front' the implication is that others in the organization follow, whereas 'leading from the centre' implies a greater involvement by others in the act of leading. It is, therefore, essential to identify where you stand in relation to the rest of the organization.

In her work on theories and practices of leadership, Coleman identifies what she calls – in a manner that is both sexist and simplistic but, nevertheless, will ring bells for many of you I'm sure – 'the great man theory' (2005: 10). Here the character of the heroic individual (often male) is the one who, leading valiantly from the front, achieves an apparently single-handed transformation of a school. The truth, however, is rarely this simple (and echoes the Fat Controller leadership style I described in the Brave Leadership section).

Another leadership attribute focused on by many researchers is that of charisma; those head teachers who seem to exert a mesmerizing hold over their school, creating significant change not by the force of their personality but by its sheer power. Conger (1989) develops tools for comparing 'charismatic' and 'non-charismatic' leaders in an attempt to remove the mysticism from leaders who are seen to create change by who they are rather than what they do. Charismatic leaders are characterized as having a strongly articulated but idealized vision combined with unconventional behaviour and a penchant for achieving their goals through unconventional means. On the other hand, the non-charismatic head agrees with the status quo and strives to maintain it, is consensus seeking and is an 'expert in using available means to achieve goals within the framework of the existing order' (1989: 51). For 'non-charismatic' read 'safe pair of hands'.

I would argue that a good head can play both roles depending on the specific needs of the school; it is just a question of remembering which one to be at any given time. However, there are some heads who seem stuck in one role or the other. These are the ones who forget that head-ship is not about them but about the school, always the school. A leader taking over a school perceived as highly successful might feel compelled to exhibit characteristics defined by Conger as 'non-charismatic', whilst the same leader trying to quickly transform a failing school into one with successful traits would have considerable difficulty adopting a set of behaviours not defined as charismatic.

Maybe we should leave the last word to the Italian researcher Sergiovanni who suggests, rather ominously, that 'the new century will not be kind to leaders who seek to change things by the sheer force of their person-ality' (2001: 38).

STEPS TO BEING BRAVE

Identify three issues you have resolved mainly though your personality and three which were solved purely by your decisions.

32 BRAVERY IS NOT FEELING YOU HAVE TO PLAY THE BIG, BRAVE HERO

No conversation about the merits or otherwise of charismatic, 'great man' leadership would be complete without reference to Sir Michael Wilshaw (one of the most favoured head teachers of both recent UK governments, left and right, and the current man in charge of England's school inspectorate, Ofsted). He, it would appear, is very much an advocate of the great man theory and has suggested that heads would be better as 'lone heroes' with characteristics modelled on Clint Eastwood's most maverick Western characters (Barker, 2011).

Successful though his career has been, this view is not generally supported by much of the current educational research. More typical, I would suggest, is the opinion of Belinda Harris (no relation No. 1) as outlined in the introduction to her book *Supporting the Emotional Work of School Leaders*. Here she describes how the 'hero head' model could actually deter quality candidates from applying for principal positions in areas of great deprivation where, rather that needing 'an extra strong' or 'super leader' the school actually needs:

> leadership that focuses on the emotional wellbeing of the school as a priority. It requires an emotionally attuned leader to create conditions of emotional safety, inclusiveness and care in which staff feel valued and supported to be creative and brave in their learning and teaching, and in which young people feel it is acceptable to learn. (Harris, 2007: 15)

> ## STEPS TO BEING BRAVE
>
> Identify an issue which will be helped by you showing your vulnerability.

33 BRAVERY IS HAVING A MORAL PURPOSE

An emotionally self-aware leader can work to ensure that the organization seeks to identify and work towards its own moral purpose, one around which all levels of staff and the wider community can gather. In his book *Leadership with a Moral Purpose*, based on his many years of experience both as a successful head in a number of challenging schools as well as working for a local authority, Ryan states that 'leadership is about a journey. It is about taking people to a defined better future. This is why vision and leadership are closely linked' (2008: 161). For him, leadership is a process that he sees as 'inside out'. In other words, it comes from within and is not based on dictates from outside.

In her work on redefining leadership, Lambert states that:

> Capacity-building principals align their actions to the belief that everyone has the right, responsibility, and capability to work as a leader. Such a perspective requires that principals be clear about their own core values and confident in their own capacity to work well with others by influencing, facilitating, guiding, and mentoring. They need to resist using authority to tell and command. (Lambert and ebrary Inc., 2003: 11)

This would appear to add more weight to the headship models I have described as the Nurturer and the Gardener (see Chapters 24 and 26), especially as Lambert goes on to suggest that when principals do not act in this way they actually serve to undermine the effectiveness of the organization. This emphasizes the central role of what can be referred to as 'bringing the staff with you', an idea often mentioned in writing about change. My Corporate Executives and Fat Controllers would probably argue that they agree with the need to do this, but would actually go about ensuring staff loyalty in a more, let's say direct way.

> Leadership is about taking people to a defined better future.

STEPS TO BEING BRAVE

If the school were to erect a memorial to you after you've gone and inscribe on it your 'moral purpose', write down what you think it would say.

34 BRAVERY IS NOT BEING SCARED TO SHOW YOUR PASSION

If you go to work and find that you are experiencing 'any kind of feeling by which the mind is powerfully affected or moved' then, according to the *Oxford English Dictionary*, you are experiencing something called 'passion'. And rightly so. In their authoritative work on the subject, Day and Leithwood give examples of where they see this characteristic in its leader as a major part of a school's transformation:

> Like effective teachers, these principals had a passion for their school, a passion for their students and a passionate belief that who they were and how they led could make a difference to the lives of staff, students, parents and the community, both in the moments of leadership and the days, weeks, months and even years afterwards. (Day and Leithwood, 2007: 176)

Whilst not every member of the school community is able to agree on what 'passion' is in a school leader, they would all agreed that it is something they would want that leader to have.

STEPS TO BEING BRAVE

Share your own passions and then encourage all your staff to identify five things in education they are passionate about.

35 BRAVERY IS NOT ACCEPTING THE STATUS QUO

Building on the idea of the passionate school leader, Day and Leithwood (2007) also studied the various ways that principals sustain their 'emotional investment' in a school. The key factor in many of these cases was the principal's determination not to accept the status quo under any circumstances. Passionate that a difference needed to be made, and determined to be the one who could make that difference, they would actively and professionally challenge the attitudes, behaviours and beliefs that were prevalent in the organization and that were, up to that point, holding it back from making any progress.

The role of school leader is always 'full on' – it is possible to allow every minute of every day to be filled by the minutia of school life. When your life is filled with issues such as litter, toilets, attendance figures, electricity failures and e-mail filtering (to name just five off the top of this head's head) it is very easy to lose sight of the fact that your job isn't just to deal with what is but what could be. Bravery is forcing yourself to look at the horizon, beyond the clutter and create the space to ensure your school moves past the status quo and in the direction it needs to go.

STEPS TO BEING BRAVE

Imagine no one in your school makes any decision for the next year. Left to drift, describe what the school would be like.

36 BRAVERY IS PORTRAYING YOURSELF AS THE LEAD LEARNER

Heads should see themselves as responsible for the organization-wide expectation of learning, setting the tone for being the head of a learning school. These head teachers create an expectation of high achievement in both staff and students when it comes to learning and building internal capital and capacity, and therefore should be seen as lead learners. In fact, I always worry about the know-it-all attitude of some principals. I am far more drawn to those who admit their fallibility and openly want to learn. In my own case, for example, I've had pupils teach me sign language, which is a very clear advert for the type of approach I wish everyone in the organization to embrace. Our leadership group meets regularly to learn together with some of the great thinkers of our day. This clearly sets the agenda for all adults in the building to be information gatherers and appliers and not simply dispensers of knowledge.

> ### STEPS TO BEING BRAVE
>
> Start the next meeting you chair by describing the most important thing you have learned in the last week and identify what you hope to learn in the next week. Ask each person around the table to do the same.

37 BRAVERY IS NOT BEING ONE-DIMENSIONAL

Much of the research focuses on the various leadership structures that can be used to bring about effective change in a school. Having a leadership structure is one thing; but this structure actually moving the school forward – and together – is another thing completely.

In his work, *Leading the Learning Organization,* Belasen suggests that the style of leadership structure used is key to an organization's ability to be successful in the long term:

> Tall, hierarchically structured organizations can run through midlevel, transactional managers who rely on the exchange of rewards for performance. The vision of these transactional managers begins and ends with performance and results, not with performance break-through and results. (Belasen, 2000: 3)

The structure works but the organization this structure is holding up is flawed. Yes, there are certain short-term activities that need to be used and measured, but if that is all the structure can do then that is as far as school change goes. To draw on my analogy from the Brave Choices section, you will be forever sprinting. Marathon activities that actually create significant and lasting school change take a different sort of structure.

STEPS TO BEING BRAVE

Identify three leadership decisions which you will delegate completely to someone else.

38 BRAVERY IS RECOGNIZING THE BALANCE BETWEEN THE WHO AND THE WHAT

A school leader's job is successful to the extent to which he or she gets right the subtle interplay between dealing with people and dealing with, well, stuff. In detailed case studies covering four countries, Mulford and colleagues conclude that the first necessary steps in creating meaningful organizational change is 'developing common understandings, honesty and trust through dialogue, sharing and distributed leadership, plus managing the inevitable risk and conflict involved' (Mulford et al., 2003: 189). This, clearly, is the people stuff and is important to get right. But there are also the organizational and technical details to identify and improve. Dimmock and Walker (2005) outline the three categories of skills they believe are *de rigueur* for all successful principals:

- Personal – how a leader manages his or her own behaviours and thoughts in their professional life.

- Communicative and influence – how a leader interacts at an interpersonal level with colleagues and other members of the community. In particular, how they mobilize colleagues and other school community members to a sustained commitment to school improvement.

■ Organizational and technical – this relates to the techniques, strategies and systems that are associated with creating and sustaining school improvement.

They go on to observe:

> The key skills essential to running good schools and colleges are personal and interpersonal on the one side, and technical and task-oriented on the other. It is the achievement of high levels of both, and a balance between the two, that distinguishes effective leaders. (Dimmock and Walker, 2005: 163)

STEPS TO BEING BRAVE

For each of the ability areas – personal, communication and influence, organizational and technical – identify how you have shown ability and also what you need to improve.

39 BRAVERY IS ADMITTING WHEN YOU DON'T KNOW THE MEANING OF A LONG WORD

Sometimes, in amongst all the research and words of wisdom about what to do in order to be an effective and courageous leader, it is easier for a researcher to simply say what *not* to do. In *The Six Secrets of Change*, school leadership überguru Michael Fullan states:

> One of the ways not to develop capacity is through criticism, punitive consequences, or what I more comprehensively call judgmentalism. Judgmentalism is not just seeing something as unacceptable or ineffective. It is that, but it is particularly harmful when it is accompanied by pejorative stigma. (Fullan, 2008: 58)

STEPS TO BEING BRAVE

Have a 'long word of the week' which you display on the staffroom wall along with its meaning.

40 BRAVERY IS GIVING PERMISSION TO PEOPLE TO LIVE A NEW STORY

Fullan goes on to offer advice, particularly for new leaders, to 'invest in capacity building while suspending short-term judgment' (2008: 58). Now, the first element of this is clear enough. Of course you need to plan to make a school capable of more than it is currently. In *Improving Schools in Exceptionally Challenging Circumstances*, Harris (another no-relation I promise) and colleagues conclude that 'in addition to building personal capacity, the Heads also recognised interpersonal capacity and organisational capacity as important elements of raising attainment' (2006: 150). Raising attainment (i.e. scores) may well be the lever that is used by politicians to pull the appropriate financial levers, but it clearly must not be the single focus of the school principal who is seeking meaningful enduring transformation. This is backed up by Hargreaves and Fink who conclude their chapter on sustainable leadership with the following:

> If the quest to improve achievement rests on cynical strategies to raise test scores, the results will be educationally unsupportable and unsustainable. Apparent improvements will largely be temporary and quickly reach a plateau; they will register as improvements only in what is directly tested. (Hargreaves and Fink, 2007: 46–64)

They conclude that 'improvement needs energy' and call for increased financial and human resources to be committed to making major change. Helping the school grow as a whole and across all aspects of school life is key, not just chasing the most number of those dreaded and dreadful KPIs that I talk about in the Brave Politics section.

So, building capacity is a given but what about the second part of Fullan's statement – to suspend short-term judgement? This is where the challenge lies, especially in situations such as the one I found myself in when I arrived at NUSA. If you are brought in to turn around a school that, according to a whole host of measures, is a failing one, it is obvious to assume that everything and everyone there is failing and that the first thing you should do is clear the decks. Nowhere is this pressure greater than when you consider what you should do about the existing teaching team. It would not seem to be an unfair assumption to put the school's failings down to them – along with the management team you are inheriting – and have the word 'cull' at the top of your school improvement to-do list.

I inherited around 60% of the staff of the previous school but I can assure you that Fullan's words are true. Rather than focus on what they *hadn't been able to do* I made the conscious decision to concentrate on what they *would be able to do* in the new school with new leadership, new opportunities and a whole new ethos across the organization as a whole. I retained my staff and leadership team despite the protestations from my lords and masters at the Department for Education who were in favour of the short-term, headline-grabbing cull approach. I am delighted not only to have created living proof that Fullan is right but also to have vindicated my long-held belief that everybody wants to do a good job, and more often than not simply needs the right sort of support from the top in order to achieve this.

> Everybody wants to do a good job, and more often than not simply needs the right sort of support from the top in order to achieve this.

This support often takes the form of permission to do the right thing by the children, as Thomson emphasizes in *Schooling the Rustbelt Kids*. She highlights the central role of the principal in setting the climate for change within a school:

> In each of the schools where there is an explicit equity agenda for reform, it is the Principal who 'gives permission' within the school. While individual teachers can take up questions of curriculum and pedagogy, if there is a passionate and committed Principal then equity and 'doing justice' still matter across the institution. (Thomson, 2002: 162)

This chimes true with the process at NUSA, where I have on many occasions felt myself to be the parent giving permission for my child to take a risk, to go places they have never been before. I have openly modelled brave behaviour and encouraged staff to engage in wonder and fun as credible tools in their armoury.

STEPS TO BEING BRAVE

Ensure you can identify and celebrate examples of risk taking within your staff.

41 BRAVERY IS REMINDING EVERY ADULT THAT EVERY CHILD SHOULD BE AT THE CENTRE OF THE CHANGE

Changes that do not have a positive effect – directly or indirectly – on student outcomes are simply window-dressing. Great, positive change could be happening within a school, but it is vital that this change touches the student body in a way in which they can engage. In the early days of involvement with the predecessor school I saw pupils, when informed of a new initiative, frequently assume that the change was not for them. Some even assumed the new building was for other children and that they would end up having to go elsewhere.

It is essential pupils realize that the changes taking place in the school, *their school*, are for them; that they are at the centre of all the efforts being undertaken to make things better. One way to achieve this is to focus all efforts around the core theme of *learning* – everything is being done to make the learning better, more effective, more enjoyable and more engaging. As Alexander and Potter state: 'A culture of learning has to actively engage people in the joy of learning, and the experience of it' (2005: 35).

One of the common features of failing schools is the way in which the children do not feel valued. Around this central theme of 'the joy of learning' there must be a genuine push to ensure children feel valued and secure, that the staff – *all* staff – genuinely care for them and want them to be happy and work well (in that order).

To move from a situation where children are the problem ('Kids from round here') to an acceptance that the professional responsibility of every single teacher is to genuinely care for all children to bring the best out of them, now that's a transformation.

> **STEPS TO BEING BRAVE**
>
> Meet a selection of pupils every month for refreshments and a chat. Ask the pupils what they are pleased with and what they wish was changed about the school.

42 BRAVERY IS GIVING THE PUPILS REAL POWER TO CHANGE THEIR SCHOOLING

Almost every summary of effective schools contains frequent mentions of the elevated place the learner must have in that institution. Wrigley describes a vision based on school improvement in which all schools must be:

- A place where everybody is welcome, where learners and teachers are accepted in their individuality.

- A place where people are allowed time to grow up, to take care of one another and be treated with respect. (Wrigley, 2003: 5)

At NUSA we have grown our involvement of pupils from the early seeds when we used them to help design the new school uniform and even choose the supplier, through their involvement in hundreds of staff selection interviews (myself included), to the formation of a peer coun-selling team who work directly with the adult teams to solve issues including bullying and misbehaviour.

> Pupils should be encouraged to partici-pate in the running and organisation of their school.

STEPS TO BEING BRAVE

Set aside £2,000 to be spent by your Pupil Council to improve learning.

43 BRAVERY IS RELEASING THE TRAPPED ENERGY OF YOUR SCHOOL

In *How to Improve Your School*, Brighouse and Woods state that 'the first rule of leadership is that it is shared' (1999: 32). They argue strongly that leadership should be not just the domain of the head or even of the leadership team. Rather, it should be distributed further to reach the staff and the learners themselves. In this way, leadership is not some-thing done to the staff and the children but by them.

As Hargreaves says:

In short, in the work on student voice and staff co-construction we find a model of new forms of leadership and partnership that covers the three elements in our definition of system leadership:

- Agreement about the purposes of education

- Partnership in the design and operation of the school

- Agreement on how the quality of teaching and learning is judged. (Hargreaves, 2007: 18)

Between them, Brighouse, Woods and Hargreaves call for an open and clear approach to change, where pupils and staff share in the process. The image of releasing rather than restricting energy is a powerful metaphor for the demands faced by schools needing to transform their educational outcomes. Staff want to feel they are being led, but it is a mistake for a head to assume this gives them the permission to adopt a 'tour guide' approach, leading from the front, umbrella in hand, occasionally slowing down to explain the view to the followers. I believe that leadership is more about helping others to see the possibility of their journey and to identify where we are all travelling, rather than fostering the passivity caused by the tour guide. The energy released by encouraging staff and children to be amongst a school's 'trailblazers' as opposed to mere travellers is immense. And as such, the journey is far more likely to succeed.

> Leadership should be not just the domain of the head or even of the leadership team.

> ## STEPS TO BEING BRAVE
>
> Once a term invite pupils to present their views to the leadership team of your school.

44 BRAVERY IS ACCEPTING RESPONSIBILITY FOR HAVING HAPPY STAFF

Next time you are in a meeting with a group of heads, ask for a show of hands relating to whether they want all their staff to be happy and effective. This is clearly a no-brainer; notwithstanding Sir Michael Wilshaw's claim that 'if anyone says to you that "staff morale is at an all-time low" you will know you are doing something right'.

Reid and colleagues state: 'It is crucial for schools to be well-managed organisations. In this context, a "happy", efficient staff is of key importance' (1987: 224). That said, the staff you inherit bring with them a whole set of hopes, beliefs and expectations that can play a major part in the success or otherwise of the transformation you are hoping to achieve. After all, like you and the students, the staff are on their own journey.

Another query to put to your fellow heads is this one: 'Hands up who is prepared to take direct responsibility for personally ensuring that all their staff are both effective *and* happy.' This might elicit more of a mixed response, if your peers are being honest.

The key to school-wide happiness seems to be to bring everyone's journey in line with the one you are setting out for the school, and then ensure they are all happy travellers. After all, their satisfaction levels will clearly affect the speed of change possible. Barth observes:

> A good school for me is one where each adult has chosen to be. Pupils live under a compulsory attendance law. They must come to school. Most adults feel every bit as conscripted. Yet, we all know that people who are going through the motions do not make very good teachers. (Barth, 1990: 162)

How do they get to achieve these levels of happiness? The answer is in the quote above by Reid and colleagues: being 'well-managed'. That is to say, the school leader has put in place procedures and activities that will bring people together in a positive and uplifting way. As Reid et al. go on to explain, when it comes to achieving staff happiness: 'operating on agreed, united policies appear to be the most effective' (1987: 12).

What's more, as many teachers originally entered the profession filled with a desire to be part of some form of educational transformation, Barth (1990) suggests that the crisis in education is less about *commitment* to education than *recommitment* to it. To what extent are you using the lever of a whole new school journey to help recommit staff to the very thing they came into the job for in the first place? Measuring the happiness levels in your staff will give you a clear indication as to how well you are doing that as a leader.

STEPS TO BEING BRAVE

Introduce a 'staff star' award. Staff nominate colleagues who 'go the extra mile' to be helpful. Ensure all nominated staff are congratulated and/or rewarded.

45 BRAVERY IS FACING UP TO THE FACT THAT POOR STAFF BEHAVIOUR MAY SIMPLY BE A REFLECTION OF POOR LEADERSHIP

I have overheard some crass comments in the principals' 'locker room' about poor staff attitudes, rarely giving thought to the fact that poor staff attitude might be the result of poor leadership. When any criticism of staff behaviour is mentioned amongst our leadership team I always ask them the following question: 'What mistake have we made to cause this behaviour?' Not only does this ensure we are always reflecting on our own actions, it also serves to remind everyone that good leadership, like good teaching, is all about relationships.

> Good leadership, like good teaching, is all about relationships.

The nature of the relationships formed within any organization will clearly have an impact on the final outcomes. It is debatable whether strong relationships come from effective leadership or effective leadership results from strong relationships, but the importance of the relationship itself is beyond debate. As Sizer states in his foreword to Barth's *Improving Schools from Within:*

> Build a school on honest relationships, and the inept, confused, or slothful teacher will be exposed, unable to hide in her or his classroom. Create a climate of trust, and insecure teachers will develop confidence with the help of their colleagues. Put bluntly, a collegial school drives out incompetents and succours the temporarily weak. Strong teachers elicit the best from students and guide them in serious learning. (Sizer, 1990: xii)

Barth himself is convinced that the most important relationship within a school that requires change is that between principal and teacher:

> If the teacher-principal relationship can be characterised as helpful, supportive, trusting, revealing of craft knowledge, so too will others. To the extent that teacher-principal interactions are suspicious, guarded, distant, adversarial, acrimonious or judgemental, we are likely to see these traits pervade the school. The relationship between teacher and principal seems to have an extraordinary amplifying effect. It models what all relationships will be. (Barth, 1990: 170)

Barth would almost certainly have difficulty supporting the models of headship I describe as the Fat Controller or Corporate Executive. It is important however to emphasize that Barth's work does not suggest that the collegial principal is weak; it is possible to be helpful and supportive whilst still offering very clear direction.

STEPS TO BEING BRAVE

List the three things that have annoyed you most about the behaviour of staff from other schools. Now identify what actions of yours could have improved this.

46 BRAVERY IS FOCUSING ON GOOD TEACHING AND HELPING TEACHERS ASPIRE TO IT

There is a growing bank of evidence that emphasizes the direct link between the quality of teaching and the outcome of pupils. The movement away from more traditional, didactic forms of teaching has thrown up the need for improved discussion about what makes a good twenty-first century teacher and how schools best go about implementing the most effective techniques. Trigwell and colleagues confidently demonstrate that:

> in the classes where teachers describe their approach to teaching as having a focus on what they do and on transmitting knowledge, students are more likely to report that they adopt a surface approach to the learning of that subject. Conversely, but less strongly, in the classes where students report adopting significantly deeper approaches to learning, teaching staff report adopting approaches to

> teaching that are more oriented towards students and to changing the students' conceptions. (Trigwell et al., 1999: 13)

As Clarke observes, it is important to remember that teaching and learning do not occur in a bubble isolated from the daily interactions of the school, but are part of every interaction: 'While a focus on teaching and learning is crucial, this does, of course, mean that the conditions must be in place in which effective teaching can occur' (2005: 96).

The good school leader will do whatever it takes to ensure that the quality of teaching and learning are the number one focus of all the professionals within the school. You may not be able to influence every lesson taking place on a daily basis, but you certainly can make a significant impact on the conditions within which those lessons take place.

That said, this comes with a note of warning to schools that only focus change on the performance and skill of their teachers. Whilst this may be the most important part of the process, if considered in isolation there is a real danger that staff will feel victimized and 'done too' rather than active agents of change.

> The good school leader will do whatever it takes to ensure that the quality of teaching and learning are the number one focus of all the professionals within the school.

STEPS TO BEING BRAVE

Ensure every staff briefing and every meeting contain reference to effective teaching and learning.

47 BRAVERY IS MAKING SURE YOU MEET PARENTS MORE THAN HALFWAY

Parents play a huge part in the lives of the children in your school, for better or for worse. In areas of socio-economic deprivation and a history of inferior quality schooling, that role can tend to be a negative one. The experiences that parents – and the extended family – had at school and in life subsequently may have been quite poor and this negativity is transferred to their children. Clarke points out the likelihood that 'many parents/carers would themselves have had negative experiences of school' and his research clearly shows that this experience has a marked impact on outcomes: 'Only 30% of the children of unskilled manual parents achieve 5 GCSE (A*–C) grades compared to 59% of the children of managerial or professional parents' (2005: 167).

While few would argue that isolating parents from the learning of their offspring to protect the children's life chances is the way forward, the current approach of simply informing them about their child's behaviour and progress via a barrage of data thrown down a one-way street can be unhelpful or even destructive. Wrigley warns that much of the current legislation does assume a one-way relationship between school and parents:

> The school's statutory responsibility to report on a child's attainment supports the consumer relationship, but not an active partnership in supporting learning. Both sides can feel threatened; teachers become suspicious of parents, who appear to take on the role of watchdogs. (Wrigley, 2003: 147)

He concludes that this is 'hardly a basis on which to establish a trusting partnership'.

One of the obstacles to improved relationships between home and school is – or can be if you let it – the 'league table' mentality. While it is clear that the publishing of comparative examination results can lead to judgement and blame between communities, it is always possible to find some domain in which a community's achievements can be celebrated. Maybe your school has the highest number of Grade 3 nose flute players? Who cares what it is as long as it can be celebrated in some way. Whatever the success, don't waste the opportunity to mark how well your pupils are doing; after all, nothing breeds success like success! Most heads have discovered that having a rich source of data about student achievement has been very useful, and has enabled dialogues, rather than accusations, to start.

> The brave leader welcomes all interactions with parents and treats them as the school's biggest ally.

While so many schools seem content to have parents as their adversaries, the brave leader welcomes all interactions with them and treats them as the school's biggest ally. Rather than ever allowing the relationship to become one based on mistrust and anger, they work to ensure that parent–school relationships are entirely focused on collaborating to create the climate for pupil success. It has been too easy for young people to exploit the gap between parents and school to their own benefit; I have seen the colour drain from the face of one 'artful dodger' who suddenly realized that his parents and teachers were working together!

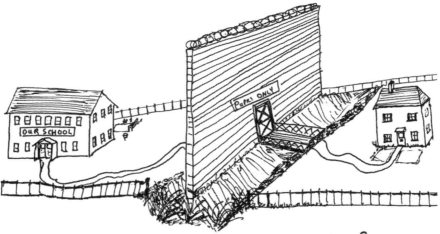

IS THERE A CLEAR VIEW BETWEEN SCHOOL + HOME?

STEPS TO BEING BRAVE

List five innovative ways you could improve school contact with parents.

48 BRAVERY IS HAVING THE COURAGE TO INVOLVE THE COMMUNITY IN YOUR SUCCESS AS A SCHOOL LEADER

Evidence that positive relationships can be formed even in the most strained conditions are outlined in the research we met earlier by Thomson (2002) in her study of the work of principals in challenging communities in Australia. Looking at an area known as the 'rustbelt' (a region created under the boom of car production, now a centre of mass unemployment and despondency), Thomson interviewed a number of head teachers, several of whom were leading schools that were seen as 'beacons of light' in an otherwise depressed area. The thread of similarity she found between the leaders was their passion for engaging with their community. They were often prepared to focus on the smallest of opportunities for partnership to ensure the relationship took hold.

A 'local' school (as opposed to one whose pupils come from a scattered geographical area) will naturally reflect the issues, challenges and successes of that community. And rightly so. Even with the extended school agenda, enabling many pupils to be in the school building for over ten hours a day, the single biggest effect on pupils' beliefs and opinions will inevitably come from the community and home. (Although admittedly parents do not always recognize this: I was told of a mother pleading with a French teacher to make her daughter behave better at home. The French teacher only saw the girl for three hours a week.)

Sheldon and Epstein carried out research across forty-nine schools into the effect on behaviour made by strong community partnership programmes. They discovered a greater improvement in pupil behaviour for schools that had behaviour strategies and good community links compared with those which solely focused on the behaviour itself: 'The results suggest that creating more connections and greater consistency within school, family, and community contexts may be one way for schools to improve student behaviour and school discipline' (2002: 17).

> Creating more connections and greater consistency within school, family, and community contexts may be one way for schools to improve student behaviour and school discipline.

I knew this intuitively and also through my previous experience as a head, so when I arrived at NUSA such activities were high on my list. However, the pressure on me from the Department for Education *not* to focus on engagement in community-based activities was huge. Their twisted logic seemed to be: How can you improve grades inside a school by focusing on activities outside it? This pressure became all the more intense when Ofsted decided they were going to drop the community-based aspect of the inspection. 'School improvement is about what goes in inside the school' was the message coming at me from all sides and it took all my bravery, matched with my own winning charm and natural belligerence, to resist the pressure. What's more, and this is something I would recommend to all head teachers, by having a research-backed approach to my work I knew that I was doing more than just following a hunch. Observations like Sheldon and Epstein's really help to keep you going when you are faced with one of these 'emperor's new clothes' situations.

In general, the hardest part is admitting that something isn't working and then seeking help to make things better. At times it can be easy to become trapped in a sequence of blame where every party – the school, the teachers, the children, the parents, the community, the politicians, the newspapers – all blame each other. While this cycle can be extremely destructive, Pialoux and Beaud advise that although it may be painful to make visible the social suffering of a school's community it is 'also liberating for those who had thought it was their fault' (1999: 259).

Being part of a healthy community makes for healthy members of that community, so it is worth going through the pain of admitting it when things aren't right.

A school that positions itself at the heart of the community is well placed to help that community thrive, with benefits for everyone in the short term as well as the longer term. Of course, appreciating that community involvement is the right thing to do and knowing how to do community involvement well are two separate issues. When schools set out to involve their local communities there can be a real danger that the process is entered into with an unrealistic view of the day-to-day challenges faced by the pupils and parents within that area. Wrigley observes:

> Unless we learn to connect with the experience of poverty, our school improvement efforts will fail to engage creatively with the challenge of raising achievement. The general message so far from official channels has been to reinforce the boundaries between school and community in the interest of minimising distractions to school learning. (Wrigley, 2003: 139)

However, it is worth the effort needed to get it right and, as the leader, although you can't do it on your own, you are the only one who can genuinely move the process forward. And when it does happen, despite misguided assertions to the contrary by people who should know better (or so you'd think), the benefits within the school are enormous.

> **STEPS TO BEING BRAVE**
>
> Write the local newspaper article you would like to read about your school. Identify how you can move towards making it a reality.

49 BRAVERY IS NOT TRYING TO FIND SOMEONE TO BLAME

Defining where leadership responsibilites start and end is an area of great interest for most leaders, particularly those who face making transformation within a community. Understanding how leadership brings about change, and how previously ineffective leadership teams can be transformed into wonderfully successful ones, is at the heart of the process. It is interesting that some researchers have tried to play down the importance of leadership on school outcomes. Sergiovanni starts his book on moral leadership in this way:

> Leadership is not a magic solution for improving schools. Moreover, focusing on leadership separately from such issues as school governance, finance, parental involvement, curriculum reform, labour relations, diversity, teaching and learning, and assessment may

cover up problems and provide symptomatic relief that makes us feel good but changes little that matters. (Sergiovanni, 1992: 1)

Whilst I understand Sergiovanni's viewpoint, it would be equally wrong to dismiss the importance of leadership attitudes simply because many other factors are also at work. Those same factors were at work under the previous leadership so something must have changed. The balance is to strike the line between the 'hero heads' who think they can change everything using willpower and professional brute force (i.e. the carrot and stick approach but deploying both items to hit people with if they don't perform), and those who blame mitigating circumstances for nothing changing at all.

I believe it can be very useful to take the blame when things aren't going well as it galvanizes you into action (the buck stops here and all that) but it is equally important to not always take the credit when it goes well. You know they know. They know you know. But what matters is that everyone can feel they have played a part in making something become wonderful.

STEPS TO BEING BRAVE

Identify something good you have taken responsibility for in the past year. Think of ways you could spread the credit to others.

50 BRAVERY IS GIVING YOUR LEADERSHIP AWAY

As all good teachers know, the best way to get respect is to give respect. It is the same with leadership. If you want a great team all heading forward in the same direction under their own impetus (as opposed to being dragged uphill by a lonely and exasperated school leader) then they need to feel part of the process of change and believe they have at least some say in how that change is to be achieved.

> The best way to get respect is to give respect.

As soon as you embark upon a process of distributed leadership you start to see a symbiotic relationship emerging between the leadership team and the principal. This practically guarantees increased levels of support for the head and a greater buy-in by the leadership team, who genuinely start to see themselves as part of the solution as well as developing the necessary leadership skills that will serve to increase capacity across the school and into the future.

According to Earley and Weindling, distributed leadership is to be found in every successful organization:

> Leadership is dispersed throughout the whole organisation and it is not the leader but leadership that is the key factor. Today's leadership needs to be decentralised and distributed in every part of the

organisation so those on the periphery who are first to spot challenges can act instantly on them. (Earley and Weindling, 2004: 15)

Are you brave enough to create a whole team of leaders yet still retain responsibility for personally ensuring the work gets done, the changes happen and great progress is made? After all, you know where the buck stops …

STEPS TO BEING BRAVE

Draw your leadership diagram in a way that doesn't emphasize you are the boss!

51 BRAVERY IS WORKING WITH THE PEOPLE YOU HAVE RATHER THAN THE ONES YOU WISH YOU HAD

In his work on human development, Dr Clare Graves expanded on his theory of human development: the Emergent, Cyclical, Double-Helix Model of the Adult Human Biopsychosocial Systems, presented in his Spiral Dynamics© trainings and materials. He believed this point of view had implications for the way organizations are led:

In this system, management is based on the assumption that people have unequal competences and capacities and unequal needs … in this system, the means to the end or organisational goals are restructured to fit the individual characteristics of the organisational

> member, rather than attempts to restructure the person to fit the organisational needs. The manager's role is to rework the organisa- tion so that its goals are achieved utilising people as they are, not as some one wishes them to be, or perceives they should be. (Graves, 1981: 8)

I have seen this in action in all my leadership roles – very few people come to work wishing to be mediocre, if any. Most of us want to be a success, and to be seen as such. I have known teachers who clearly were once leading lights, with bags of energy and potential, yet who have become hollow shells of their former selves. When I investigated what had happened to cause this demise, it was often that they felt themselves victims of the system, as if the school had tried to make them become someone else. I think the most rewarding part of my job is in helping individuals (the clue is in the word – 'individual') to find their own voice in the school. You don't have to compromise on your long-term journey just because you agree to get there in a different way. Allowing someone to contribute through their passion and skills, rather than sup- pressing them to fit your predetermined plan, is a no-brainer to me.

STEPS TO BEING BRAVE

List all your leadership team and by each name describe their greatest asset.

52 BRAVERY IS SOMETIMES BEING A SIMPLE PRINCIPAL

Margaret Wheatley, in her popular work analysing the leadership of business organizations, *Leadership and the New Science*, likens them to 'fractals' or self-replicating pockets of behaviour (which may be positive or negative):

> Self-similarity is achieved not through compliance to an exhaustive set of standards and rules, but from a few simple principles that everyone is accountable for, operating in a condition of individual freedom. (Wheatley, 2006: 148)

I repeat this quote because it is important. I also use it on the front page of my staff handbook and as the backdrop to many a meeting. Schools are complex places; each day, hundreds of young people and adults doing unexpected things in unpredictable ways. To write a set of rules to govern this is not only impractical, it is also very stupid. When the unexpected happens we want the adults to calmly apply simple principles to guide a solution, not turn to the index of a 100-page rule book. I think the KISS concept (Keep It Simple Stupid) should be adhered to more closely in education because we are all guilty of making some very basic ideas extremely complicated, either to make ourselves look good or in some instances (and you know who you are!) to make bags of money.

STEPS TO BEING BRAVE

Describe three simple principles that you would like your school to be run by.

53 BRAVERY IS KNOWING THAT A TEAM IS A COLLECTION OF INDIVIDUALS

The successful leader must have a good grasp of human interaction in all its complexity and frustration. A remote principal, one who is considered to be without empathy, will find it difficult to harness the skills of a large group of staff. As Shaw notes on the cultural context of educational leadership: 'Successful leaders rely heavily on human relationships. They need to understand how X will react, what motivates Y, or why Z did that when confronted by W' (2005: 45).

This is where successful leadership grows – in the understanding of individual interactions, of individuals interacting with other individuals and of being prepared to understand and accommodate this collaborative process. Sometimes the very best ideas can fail to take hold, not because there is anything wrong with them but because of the leader's lack of understanding regarding the individuals who are expected to engage with and then deliver the initiative in question.

STEPS TO BEING BRAVE

Draw a 'relationship web' for your leadership team, connecting their roles and interactions.

54 BRAVERY IS KNOWING YOU DON'T HAVE TO DO IT ALONE

In *School Improvement for Real,* another of the leadership academic heavyweights, David Hopkins, states:

> In a nutshell, top-down direction and institutional hierarchies are antithetical to democracy in action. Multiple partnerships, with variable leadership, offer a more appropriate set of norms, and are more likely to impact upon classrooms and student learning. (Hopkins, 2000: 121)

There are numerous opportunities and demands offered though new models of partnership, as Fullan points out in his authoritative book *Leadership and Sustainability* (2005). He believes that the only way to successfully build capacity – both laterally and vertically – in a school is through partnerships and networks. This, he stresses, can only occur if there is not only a new sort of leader but also a 'critical mass of leaders' who share a common understanding of the benefit of this type of work. In other words, if sufficient numbers of heads work to create a new culture of school improvement that draws on a collaborative, distributed model both within and between schools.

STEPS TO BEING BRAVE

Embark on at least one new partnership with another school.

55 BRAVERY IS KNOWING WHEN A BANNER IS JUST A BANNER

> If four outstanding principals hang the same banner in the cafeteria – 'All students can learn' – I might conclude that one key to effective leadership is an inspiring banner in the lunchroom. However if two of the less effective leaders display the same banner, I would reconsider my conclusion. The banner alone does not guarantee success. Of course, this doesn't mean that no principal should hang a banner, or that each principal must mimic every behaviour of the very effective ones. But the practices of great principals do not get in the way of their success and others can learn from them. (Whitaker, 2003: 4)

Without wishing to get into an argument with Bananarama, Whitaker's remark would suggest that it *is* what you do, as well as the way that you do it, that can make the difference. Some leaders explain their success as 'gut feeling' or 'intuition'. Whilst these phenomena cannot be discounted, and do form a useful part of the arsenal of any head teacher worth his or her salt, it would be foolish to attempt transformation using these skills alone. Increasingly, schools are looking to the growing body of research to help plot strategies that will successfully steer them through the ever more complex world in which schools operate. But this success involves an interplay between what is done and how it is done.

As Whitaker suggests, doing the right things is only part of the battle, as is doing things right. Doing the right things right is the answer combined with the acuity to know what they are and the bravery to follow through on them in the right way. Nothing to it really ...

56 BRAVERY IS KNOWING THE HUGE IMPACT YOUR ACTIONS WILL HAVE ON LEARNING

Unless leadership impacts on learning it is missing its core purpose. Sometimes it is possible for institutions to become so focused on the structures and procedures of leadership that they lose sight of the very reason they exist. Professor John West-Burnham, who is a guest member of our leadership team, introduced us to a quadrant approach to understanding the multifaceted role of the school leader:

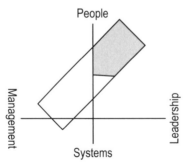

The oblong identifies the region of required working for an effective leadership team – the balancing act between leading and managing your people and your systems. The highlighted area is where a team should focus its efforts when faced with circumstances similar to the ones we found ourselves in at NUSA in the early days. In other words, leading people.

The times of greatest change can only occur with sustained effort from leading people. So, as important as systems and day-to-day management are in keeping things ticking over, change is caused by people. This is often not recognized by the powers that be – who request organizational charts and policies when you are forming a new academy rather than focusing on your methods for engaging and empowering staff. It is in resisting such pressures that your bravery is needed!

STEPS TO BEING BRAVE

Plot a chart of the last week showing how much time you spent leading and how much managing.

57 BRAVERY IS LOOKING AT YOURSELF IN THE MIRROR (ONE OF THOSE MAGNIFYING ONES THAT SHOWS UP EVERYTHING!)

West-Burnham also advocates that learning-focused leadership should have the development of reflection as a key aspect of staff practice (something that works best when the leadership focuses most upon the highlighted quadrant in the figure on page 162). In *Rethinking Educational Leadership,* he states that reflection in this area produces profound but elusive learning which is crucial for school success:

> Reflection is about self-directed, structured analysis of behaviour, ideas, situations, practice or relationships and is primarily concerned with making sense of and ordering evidence or other stimuli. The purpose of reflection is to learn from experience to inform future thinking and hence action. (West-Burnham, 2009: 116)

As NUSA is a research-based academy, we are all into collecting and analysing data. The process of carrying out effective research is like using an electron microscope on our most intimate bits; it not only scrutinizes the outside but also looks at the structures inside. This means that you can't be committed to research and be squeamish about what it shows …

> While mistakes may not be welcomed, the opportunity to reflect on them is.

The ongoing success of a process of professional reflection is that it should never turn into a witch hunt. This means that while mistakes may not be welcomed, the opportunity to reflect on them is. Any school not making mistakes on its journey is a school not taking risks, and any school not taking risks is a school that will persistently under-achieve. As Hattie, whose findings support those of West-Burnham, states:

> School leaders and teachers need to create school, staffroom and classroom environments where error is welcomed as a learning opportunity, where discarding incorrect knowledge and understandings is welcomed and where participants can feel safe to learn, re-learn and explore knowledge and understanding. (Hattie, 2008: 85)

STEPS TO BEING BRAVE

Arrange a Friday night/Saturday morning research residential for your leadership team and invite a friendly professor.

58 BRAVERY IS COLLECTING INFORMATION RATHER THAN DATA

This could be seen as a most challenging stance when viewed in the context of the current performance-driven environment encouraged by the Department for Education; where heads are being given 'extra' powers to remove unsatisfactory staff more hastily and where an analysis of success rates for every teacher and every class are automatically produced in almost every school. The challenge is to use these factors in a way that helps and motivates staff rather than alienates or stifles innovation.

Hattie identified the exponential growth of the data available to schools back in 2005 in his speech 'What is the Nature of Evidence That Makes a Difference to Learning?', in which his opening words are 'Schools are awash with data' (2005: 2). He attempts to help schools identify the important data by encouraging them to put evidence at the core of their work and ensuring the curriculum is based on evidence, as is the school development programme and any teaching and learning initiatives. He challenges schools to move from collecting more data and instead focus on 'making more defensible interpretations about teaching and learning' and to 'develop a common language about the progression of this learning as students advance through their schooling' (2005: 10). This statement, more than any other, best encapsulates the changes required at many of our most challenged schools.

The last ten years have seen us all become awash with data on teachers and pupils. The fallibility and context of this data is too often ignored. We see a list of teachers' names with their 'value added' contribution alongside it and then engage in the conversation, 'Who is best? Who is worst?' Luckily for me, I was reminded of the stupidity of this exercise when discovering the same name at both ends of the table. The context of any one nugget of data is far more complex than we ever give it credit. We happily comment to the press about why area X is lower in the GCSE league table than area Y, without ever acknowledging the fact that the two areas are completely incomparable.

The brave head needs to stand up and be counted. And remember, don't just protest when data-driven misunderstandings go against you – make an even bigger noise when it goes your way!

STEPS TO BEING BRAVE

List five items of data that you collect in your school but don't make full use of.

59 BRAVERY IS MAKING MISTAKES AND THEN LETTING OTHERS KNOW YOU MADE THEM

When Leithwood and colleagues carried out a major review of knowledge in the area of school leadership for the UK's National College of School Leadership, now the National College, they were able to distil thousands of books and papers into 'seven strong claims' (2006: 2). I have taken the liberty of putting together my own bravery-related guidance to accompany each of the claims.

1 Be brave enough to believe in the positive effect you can have.

2 Be brave enough to learn from other leaders (the successful ones!).

3 Be brave enough to adapt your practices imaginatively to fit your context (combined with being brave enough to be honest about that context in the first place).

4 Be brave enough to accept that your staff's happiness and effectiveness is your responsibility.

5 Be brave enough to share your leadership but …

6 Be brave enough to not give everything away (and astute enough to know the difference).

7 Be brave enough to look in the mirror every day and know that you, like all successful heads, are unique and have the bravery to lead uniquely.

In his large-scale and authoritative study, *How to Change 5000 Schools*, Levin concludes that

> [W]e will inevitably make mistakes in any important endeavour. The question is whether we learn from our mistakes so that subsequent performance improves. We have made many mistakes in education in the last two decades, but we have learned a great deal. We know more about the challenges to implementation and how we can address them. (Levin, 2008: 83)

STEPS TO BEING BRAVE

Write yourself a personal action plan based on points 1–7 above.

60 BRAVERY IS CARRYING ON DESPITE THE HUGE DOUBTS YOU HAVE IN YOUR ABILITY

'You can until you think you can't – and then often, you still can.' A brave head is one who, no matter how remote the prospect of change and how daunting the journey, believes that it is possible. It is someone who holds on to the dream no matter how difficult things get. And ensures others hang on to the dream too.

Headship is not a job for the faint-hearted. If you don't feel lost, desperate, unappreciated and very, very tired at least most of the time, then you must be doing something wrong! Stating your beliefs and setting the direction of your school is one of the most terrifying things you can do. You can't just believe it when you say it; you have to live it every day, and with everyone watching you – some of them, it has to be said, hoping you will fail. It is like leading a group on a foggy mountain. Everyone depends on your leadership for direction, safety and morale. While you may not have got them into this mess, you have to be the one to get them out of it. Lead them triumphantly down the hillside and great praise awaits. Make one small error and you will be left in the fog as just another failed 'super-head', doomed forever to wander through the mist looking for someone to blame.

I remember once speaking at a conference for young teachers interested in headship. Their overwhelming worry was to find out how they could avoid leading their school over the proverbial cliff and into disaster. This is what I advised them:

1   Trust your gut.

2   Ask for help.

3   If you spend your life worrying about things that may or may not happen, you *waste* it.

4   Staff are not lemmings and most won't follow you over the cliff edge anyway!

The other thing is to recognize that self-doubt is entirely natural, even among the bravest appearing heads. It is a sign you are human. Mortal. Genuine. If you didn't doubt your own choices or direction of travel then I don't think you would be the right material for the job anyway. Imagine a person who didn't have these doubts, who was certain they were right all the time. Is this the type of head you would want to work for?

STEPS TO BEING BRAVE

Write down three things that concern you about your leadership. Larger and bolder than this, write five things you are proud about with your leadership.

61 BRAVERY IS REJECTING THE CHEATS, SHORT CUTS AND SNAKE OIL THAT APPEAR WHEN YOU GO IN SEARCH OF THE QUICK WIN

We all want to succeed. All school leaders want to be seen to be doing well. This is partly out of a genuine desire for the school to do well and partly out of ego. The ratio of school success to ego depends on the individual head teacher.

But to succeed, and do it the way your heart tells you is right – even though it is the most difficult route from A to B – that is what takes real bravery. Not only do you have to produce the results, you have to do it in the right way. It can be very easy to be tempted into short cuts (let's call them that, 'cheats' is such a vulgar term). What should be born in mind in school leadership, as it is with promises by banks and telephone scams, is if it appears too good to be true it usually is. As more money has become available for the discretion of head teachers, the number of 'miracle solutions' has grown exponentially. So, heed my warning: watch out for the false gods, the magic bullets, the pre-packed, off-the-shelf, just-do-it-like-this-and-watch-your-school-soar systems peddled by the dubious providers that claim to deliver incredible changes in attitude and attainment.

In fact, if you get nothing else from this book then make sure you get this. There is no system. There is no short cut. There is no magic pill that will turn all your students into Oxbridge candidates and, no matter how much you manipulate the data, you cannot cheat your way to real, genuine, lasting, community-wise school improvement.

> You cannot cheat your way to real, genu-
> ine, lasting, community-wise school
> improvement.

I remember attending a talk from a purveyor of a certain magic black box that offered 'biofeedback' to help students get in the right state for learning. Along with the fancy box came a CD of calming classical music. So far so good: I see only positives in helping young people develop skills of relaxation, self-control and emotional intelligence. The warning bells really started to ring, though, when the sales pitch moved on to claims about a school which had used their system and achieved a 75% improvement in exam results, something we were told was entirely down to the magic box. When challenged about how, exactly, they knew this, they produced a spreadsheet and a supporting letter from the head of ICT at the school. So that must be OK then! They also claimed that a teacher trained in the skills of controlling their own heart-beat would, 'by symbiosis', automatically lower the heartbeats of every pupil in the class. Now at this point they certainly started to alter my heartbeat. I'm a mild man, but I am tempted to do violent things to people who promote such rubbish, especially when they try to charge £100 for equipment that costs under £5. I don't know whether a punch in the face counts as biofeedback but I was sorely tempted to find out.

Sadly, with the pressures put on heads, such pseudo-scientists and snake oil peddlers have a fertile market. Please don't be tempted. The only way to make real change is through determination and hard work and lots and lots of passion. Changing a school is tremendously demanding but recognizing the immensity of the task – and that there are no short cuts – is the first step.

> The only way to make real change is through determination and hard work and lots and lots of passion.

STEPS TO BEING BRAVE

Ask a colleague to write a paragraph about your leadership. Highlight all the positives. Give yourself a bonus mark for every time they use the word 'passion'.

62 BRAVERY IS LOOKING FOR ARGUMENTS

I once heard that Winston Churchill used to employ a close personal aide whose job it was to disagree with him. A good leader is, almost by definition, a difficult person to argue with. But a brave good leader is one who genuinely needs people to contradict, to question, to disagree, to challenge and to fight. And, if you are feeling really brave, this is something you will actively seek out in your work.

I am a big fan of using psychometric analysis or personality testing on leadership teams, not principally to control who is comes into a team but to understand better who you have in the first place. Encouraging the team to be proud of their differences and even to emphasize them when appropriate is a powerful tool for exploring the details around any problem. Some of the most exciting and productive teams I have worked with have had the ability to challenge each other vociferously over a wide range of topics. However once the heat and steam subside, a consensus is found and the team puts its combined weight behind it.

STEPS TO BEING BRAVE

Set-up a 'deliberately argumentative' chat with some of your leadership team. Ask each person to argue a point from a specific viewpoint.

63 BRAVERY IS KNOWING THAT HAVING AUTHORITY IS NOT THE SAME AS USING AUTHORITY

As the head of a school I know that pretty much what I say goes. I'm the boss. I have full authority. If I want to paint the school yellow I can. If I want to ban cabbage I can. I can do what I want and there is little you can do to stop me. However, leadership isn't about the exertion of authority but the way in which you deploy the notion of that authority. There is a world of difference between me telling a colleague what to do as a direct order and outlining the possibilities, explaining my preference and leaving the colleague with the words, 'I'm sure you'll make the right choice.'

I rarely, if ever, have had to use my full authority in a situation at school. Ironically, it is the fact that I have this authority – and everyone knows it – that means I don't have to use it. I am frequently amazed by how well people understand my desires for NUSA. Staff already know what I would say if I was consulted, 'I told them that you would be very excited/happy with/annoyed by … Is that OK?' I love to find groups of staff already trying to find an imaginative and bizarre solution to a problem I wasn't yet aware of. Believe me, giving away your authority is the securest way I know to ensure you get your way!

Giving away your authority is the securest way I know to ensure you get your way!

STEPS TO BEING BRAVE

List three ways that you will give away your authority this term.

64 BRAVERY IS YOU

When asked by Ian Gilbert to write this book, I said that I wanted to write the book that would have helped me at the lowest point of my change journey. It is difficult for me to know if I have been successful, but even if one person feels it has given them the confidence to be brave then I guess it has been a success. Real change can't happen without bravery, so please be brave – your country needs you!

A Bravery Pledge

Some think bravery is living without fear
But that is not true.
Bravery is living *despite* the fear
And doing what needs to be done
Even though you're scared to death.
Some can stand on the sidelines of life
And be content with what could have been but never was.

That is not me.
I will not look back at the end of my life
Thinking of what could have been.
I vow to live my dreams no matter what
I will stand up and be counted.

Lynn C. Johnston

STEPS TO BEING BRAVE

Write your own 'Bravery Pledge' and sign it.

STEPS TO BEING BRAVE

- Make a list of the ten things you most *fear* might happen at your school.

- Look at your list of ten things you fear. Then remember FEAR stands for False Expectations Appear Real. So now remove five that are realistically *not* going to happen.

- Write a set of 'real performance indicators' that you would like to be used for your school.

- Award a 'Brave Teacher' prize to one of your staff who has shown courage and initiative.

- Contact your local MP with a list of five things because of which he/she should be proud of your school.

- Make a presentation to your governors comparing what you want from your school with what the government seem to want.

- Ask your staff to nominate pupils for 'Genius of the Week' awards. Collate a book of your school's geniuses (or is it genii?).

- Have a theme for your learning walks within your school. Make it clear you are hoping to see examples of learning being made fun.

- Ask your staff to list three things they have taught this week which will have changed a pupil's life.

- In a meeting ask your staff to divide the school's development plan into 'sprint' or 'marathon' activities.

- Ask the community to submit stories of the area surrounding the school. Collate a book of these stories and hold a book launch.

- Identify the best thing achieved by the school in the last five years. Decide how you are going to repeat this success, but next time, even better.

- Hold a meeting between primary and secondary teachers where conversations about levels are banned. The only topic of conversation allowed is the planning of a joint project.

- Start a Cabinet of Curiosities in the entrance to your school. Encourage visitors to bring an item to be left in it.

- Hold a writing competition within your school to compose a positive poem about your school in exactly 100 words.

- Set yourself a target to hold at least one event each term that the community wouldn't expect you to!

- Ask your chef (no 'cooks' please!) to hold a Gourmet Tuesday with a menu containing unfamiliar dishes.

- Decide on at least one 'off the wall', barmy, left-field thing to do before the end of this term.

- Identify the bravest thing you have done this month. And then the stupidest. Work out why the brave one wasn't stupid and the stupid one wasn't brave!

- Write down which movie character would best match your leadership style and why.

- Identify times that you have adopted the behaviour of the Fat Controller and what happened as a result.

- Identify times that you have adopted the behaviour of the Nurturer and what happened as a result.

- Identify times that you have adopted the behaviour of the Corporate Executive and what happened as a result.

- Identify times that you have adopted the behaviour of the Gardener and what happened as a result.

- Give yourself a grade out of ten for each of the four styles of leadership that you have used in the last term. Decide if and how this balance should change over the next term.

- Circulate a short piece of academic writing to all your staff and set aside time in a meeting to discuss its implications for your school.

- Start a research board in the staffroom. Encourage staff to put interesting articles on it.

- Identify three issues you have resolved mainly though your personality and three which were solved purely by your decisions.

- Identify an issue which will be helped by you showing your vulnerability.

- If the school were to erect a memorial to you after you've gone and inscribe on it your 'moral purpose', write down what you think it would say.

- Share your own passions and then encourage all your staff to identify five things in education they are passionate about.

- Imagine no one in your school makes any decision for the next year. Left to drift, describe what the school would be like.

- Start the next meeting you chair by describing the most important thing you have learned in the last week and identify what you hope to learn in the next week. Ask each person around the table to do the same.

- Identify three leadership decisions which you will delegate completely to someone else.

- For each of the ability areas – personal, communication and influence, organizational and technical – identify how you have shown ability and also what you need to improve.

- Have a 'long word of the week' which you display on the staffroom wall along with its meaning.

- Ensure you can identify and celebrate examples of risk taking within your staff.

- Meet a selection of pupils every month for refreshments and a chat. Ask the pupils what they are pleased with and what they wish was changed about the school.

- Set aside £2,000 to be spent by your Pupil Council to improve learning.

- Once a term invite pupils to present their views to the leadership team of your school.

- Introduce a 'staff star' award. Staff nominate colleagues who 'go the extra mile' to be helpful. Ensure all nominated staff are congratulated and/or rewarded.

- List the three things that have annoyed you most about the behaviour of staff from other schools. Now identify what actions of yours could have improved this.

- Ensure every staff briefing and every meeting contain reference to effective teaching and learning.

- List five innovative ways you could improve school contact with parents.

- Write the local newspaper article you would like to read about your school. Identify how you can move towards making it a reality.

- Identify something good you have taken responsibility for in the past year. Think of ways you could spread the credit to others.

- Draw your leadership diagram in a way that doesn't emphasize you are the boss!

- List all your leadership team and by each name describe their greatest asset.

- Describe three simple principles that you would like your school to be run by.

- Draw a 'relationship web' for your leadership team, connecting their roles and interactions.

- Embark on at least one new partnership with another school.

- Make a list of the five immediate changes you would make to your school if all external constraints were removed from you.

- Plot a chart of the last week showing how much time you spent leading and how much managing.

- Arrange a Friday night/Saturday morning research residential for your leadership team and invite a friendly professor.

- List five items of data that you collect in your school but don't make full use of.

- Write yourself a personal action plan based on page 168.

- Write down three things that concern you about your leadership. Larger and bolder than this, write five things you are proud about with your leadership.

- Ask a colleague to write a paragraph about your leadership. Highlight all the positives. Give yourself a bonus mark for every time they use the word 'passion'.

- Set-up a 'deliberately argumentative' chat with some of your leadership team. Ask each person to argue a point from a specific viewpoint.

- List three ways that you will give away your authority this term.

- Write your own 'Bravery Pledge' and sign it.

BIBLIOGRAPHY

Alexander, T. and Potter, J. (2005). *Education for a Change: Transforming the Way We Teach Our Children*. London: RoutledgeFalmer.

Anderson, G. L., Herr, K. and Nihlen, A. S. (2007). *Studying Your Own School: An Educator's Guide to Practitioner Action Research*. Thousand Oaks, CA: Corwin.

Barker, I. (2011). Clint and Me: Mossbourne Head Says School Leaders Are 'Lone Heroes'. *Times Educational Supplement*, 18 February.

Barth, R. S. (1990). *Improving Schools from Within: Teachers, Parents, and Principals Can Make the Difference*. San Francisco, CA: Jossey-Bass.

Belasen, A. T. (2000). *Leading the Learning Organization: Communication and Competencies for Managing Change*. New York: State University of New York Press.

Bennett, N. and Anderson, L. (2003). *Rethinking Educational Leadership*. London: Paul Chapman.

Black, P. and Wiliam, D. (2006). *Inside the Black Box: Raising Standards through Classroom Assessment*. London: NFER Nelson.

Brighouse, T. and Woods, D. (1999). *How to Improve Your School*. London: Routledge.

Burger, J., Webber, C. F. and Klinck, P. A. (2007). *Intelligent Leadership: Constructs for Thinking Education Leaders*. Dordrecht: Springer.

Chan, T. C. (1979). *The Impact of School Building Age on Pupil Achievement. Office of School Facilities Planning.* Greenville School District, P.O. Box 2848, Greenville, SC 29602 (free).

Clarke, P. (2005). *Improving Schools in Difficulty.* London: Continuum.

Cochran-Smith, M. and Lytle, S. L. (2009). *Inquiry as Stance: Practitioner Research for the Next Generation.* New York: Teachers College Press.

Coleman, M. (2005). Theories and Practice of Leadership: An Introduction. In M. Coleman and P. Earley (eds), *Leadership and Management in Education: Cultures, Change and Context.* Oxford: Oxford University Press, pp. 6–25.

Coles, M. and Southworth, G. (2004). *Developing Leadership: Creating the Schools of Tomorrow.* Maidenhead: Open University Press.

Conger, J. A. (1989). *The Charismatic Leader: Behind the Mystique of Exceptional Leadership.* San Francisco, CA: Jossey-Bass.

Crotty, M. (1998). *The Foundations of Social Research: Meaning and Perspective in the Research Process.* London: Sage.

Day, C. (2009). *The Impact of School Leadership on Pupil Outcomes: Final Report.* London: DCSF.

Day, C. and Leithwood, K. A. (2007). *Successful Principal Leadership in Times of Change: An International Perspective.* Dordrecht: Springer.

Dimmock, C. and Walker, A. (2005). *Educational Leadership: Culture and Diversity.* London: Sage.

Doman, G. and Doman, J. (2005). *How to Teach Your Baby Math.* New York: Square One Publishing.

BIBLIOGRAPHY

Earley, P. and Weindling, D. (2004).*Understanding School Leadership.* London: Paul Chapman.

Earthman, G. I. (2004). *Prioritization of 31 Criteria for School Building Adequacy.* Baltimore, MD: American Civil Liberties Union Foundation of Maryland.

Flecknoe, M. (2001). Target Setting: Will It Help To Raise Achievement? *Educational Management Administration and Leadership,* 29, 217–228.

Fullan, M. (2005). *Leadership and Sustainability: System Thinkers in Action.* Thousand Oaks, CA: Corwin Press.

Fullan, M. (2008). *The Six Secrets of Change: What the Best Leaders Do To Help Their Organizations Survive and Thrive.* San Francisco, CA: Jossey-Bass.

Garet, M. S., Porter, A. C., Desimone, L., Birman, B. F. and Yoon, K. S. (2001). What Makes Professional Development Effective? Results from a National Sample of Teachers. *American Educational Research Journal,* 38, 915–945.

Graves, C. W. (1981). Summary Statement: The Emergent, Cyclical, Double-Helix Model of the Adult Human Biopsychosocial Systems. Handout for a presentation to the World Future Society, Boston, MA, 20 May. Available at http://www.clarewgraves.com/articles_content/1981_handout/1981_summary.pdf (accessed 17 August 2012).

Hargreaves, A. and Fink, D. (2007). Energizing Leadership for Sustainability. In Davies, B. (ed). *Developing Sustainable Leadership.* London: Paul Chapman Publishing.

Hargreaves, D. (2007). *System Re-design – 1. The Road to Transformation.* London: SSAT.

Harris, A., Clarke, P., Gunraj, J., James, B. and James, S. (2006). *Improving Schools in Exceptionally Challenging Circumstances: Tales from the Frontline.* London: Continuum.

Harris, B. (2007). *Supporting the Emotional Work of School Leaders.* London: Paul Chapman.

Harris, D. W. (2008). *Are You Dropping the Baton? From Effective Collaboration to All-Through Schools – Your Guide to Improving Transition.* Carmarthen: Crown House Publishing.

Hattie, J. (2005). What is the Nature of Evidence That Makes a Difference to Learning? Keynote address at the 2005 Australian Council for Educational Research (ACER) Conference, Melbourne, Australia, 7–9 August. Available at http://research.acer.edu.au/cgi/viewcontent.cgi?article=1008&context=research_conference_2005 (accessed 17 August 2012).

Hattie, J. (2008). *Visible Learning: A Synthesis of Over 800 Meta-Analyses Relating to Achievement.* New York: Routledge.

Hopkins, D. (2000). *School Improvement for Real.* London: RoutledgeFalmer.

Johnston, L. C. (2006). *Angel's Dance: A Collection of Uplifting and Inspirational Poetry.* Bloomington, IN: iUniverse.

Lambert, L. and ebrary Inc. (2003). *Leadership Capacity for Lasting School Improvement.* Alexandria, VA: Association for Supervision and Curriculum Development.

Leithwood, K., Day, C., Sammons, P., Harris, A. and Hopkins, D. (2006). *Seven Strong Claims about Successful School Leadership*. Nottingham: NCSL/DfES.

Levin, B. (2008). *How to Change 5000 Schools: A Practical and Positive Approach for Leading Change at Every Level*. Cambridge, MA: Harvard Education Press.

Little, J. W. (2003). Constructions of Teacher leadership in Three Periods of Policy and Reform Activism. *School Leadership and Management*, 23, 401–419.

Macbeath, J. (1998). *Effective School Leadership: Responding to Change*. London: Paul Chapman.

Martin, P. R. (2005). *Making Happy People: The Nature of Happiness and its Origins in Childhood*. London: Fourth Estate.

Menter, I. (2011). *A Guide to Practitioner Research in Education*. Thousand Oaks, CA: Sage.

Moon, B. and Shelton-Mayes, A. (1994). *Teaching and Learning in the Secondary School*. London: Routledge.

Moreno, J. M., Mulford, B. and Hargreaves, A. (2006). *Trusting Leadership: From Standards to Social Capital*. Nottingham: NCSL.

Mulford, W., Silins, H. and Leithwood, K. (2003). *Educational Leadership for Organizational Learning and Improved Student Outcomes*. Hingham, MA: Kluwer Academic Publishers.

Parkin, G. R. (1900). *Sir Edward Thring: Life, Diary and Letters*. London: Macmillan.

Pialoux, M. and Beaud, S. (1999). Permanent and Temporary Workers. In P. Bourdieu (ed.), *The Weight of the World: Social Suffering in Contemporary Society*. Oxford: Polity, pp. 257–266.

Reid, K., Hopkins, D. and Holly, P. (1987). *Towards the Effective School: The Problems and Some Solutions*. Oxford: Basil Blackwell.

Riley, K., Ellis, S., Weinstock, W., Tarrant, J. and Hallmond, S. (2006). Re-engaging Disaffected Pupils in Learning: Insights for Policy and Practice. *Improving Schools*, 9, 17–31.

Ryan, W. (2008). *Leadership with a Moral Purpose: Turning Your School Inside Out*. Carmarthen: Crown House Publishing.

Schein, E. H. (2010). *Organizational Culture and Leadership*. San Francisco, CA: Jossey-Bass.

Scribner, J. P., Sawyer, R. K., Watson, S. T. and Myers, V. L. (2007). Teacher Teams and Distributed Leadership: A Study of Group Discourse and Collaboration. *Educational Administration Quarterly*, 43, 67–100.

Sergiovanni, T. (1992). *Moral Leadership: Getting to the Heart of School Improvement*. San Francisco, CA: Jossey-Bass.

Sergiovanni, T. (2001). *Leadership: What's In It for Schools?* London: Taylor and Francis.

Shaw, M. (2005). The Cultural Context of Educational Leadership. In M. Coleman and P. Earley (eds), *Leadership and Management in Education: Cultures, Change and Context*. Oxford: Oxford University Press, pp. 26–46.

BIBLIOGRAPHY

Sheldon, S. B. and Epstein, J. L. (2002). Improving Student Behavior and School Discipline with Family and Community Involvement. *Education and Urban Society*, 35, 4–26.

Sizer, T. R. (1990). Foreword. In R. S. Barth, *Improving Schools from Within: Teachers, Parents, and Principals Can Make the Difference*. San Francisco, CA: Jossey-Bass, pp. xi–xii.

Stewart, W. (2011). New Ofsted Chief Fires Warning Shots. *Times Educational Supplement*, 13 December.

Thomas, G. (2009). *How To Do a Research Project: A Guide for Students in Education and Applied Social Sciences*. Thousand Oaks, CA: Sage.

Thomson, P. (2002). *Schooling the Rustbelt Kids: Making the Difference in Changing Times*. Stoke-on-Trent: Trentham.

Thomson, P. and Blackmore, J. (2006). Beyond the Power of One: Redesigning the Work of School Principals. *Journal of Educational Change*, 7, 161–177.

Timperley, H. and Robertson, J. (2011). *Leadership and Learning*. London: Sage.

Trigwell, K., Prosser, M. and Waterhouse, F. (1999). Relations between Teachers' Approaches to Teaching and Students' Approaches to Learning. *Higher Education*, 37, 57–70.

Watt, N. (2012). GCSE Exams to be Replace by EBacc. *The Guardian*, 17 September.

West-Burnham, J. (2009). *Rethinking Educational Leadership: From Improvement to Transformation*. London: Network Continuum.

Wheatley, M. J. (2006). *Leadership and the New Science: Discovering Order in a Chaotic World*. San Francisco, CA: Berrett-Koehler.

Whitaker, T. (2003). *What Great Principals Do Differently: Fifteen Things That Matter Most*. Larchmont, NY: Eye on Education.

Woolner, P., Hall, E., Higgins, S., McCaughey, C. and Wall, K. (2007). A Sound Foundation? What We Know about the Impact of Environments on Learning and the Implications for Building Schools for the Future. *Oxford Review of Education*, 33, 47–70.

Wrigley, T. (2003). *Schools of Hope: A New Agenda for School Improvement*. Stoke-on-Trent: Trentham.

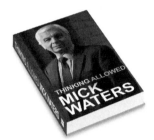

978-1-78135-056-0

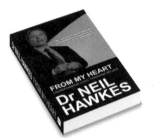

978-1-78135-106-2

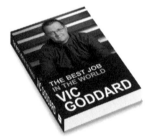

978-1-78135-110-9

Bringing together some of the most innovative practitioners working in education today

www.independentthinkingpress.com